Self Confidence for Teen Girls

CRAFTED BY SKRIUWER

Copyright © 2024 by Skriuwer.

All rights reserved. No part of this book may be used or reproduced in any form whatsoever without written permission except in the case of brief quotations in critical articles or reviews.

For more information, contact : **kontakt@skriuwer.com** (www.skriuwer.com)

TABLE OF CONTENTS

CHAPTER 1: UNDERSTANDING CONFIDENCE

- Explains the true meaning of confidence
- Shows how self-esteem and self-worth affect daily life
- Discusses influences like family, school, and media
- Offers practical steps to begin building confidence

CHAPTER 2: WHY CONFIDENCE MATTERS FOR TEEN GIRLS

- Highlights the role of confidence in relationships and school success
- Shows how it impacts body image and mental health
- Provides real-life examples of confidence boosting opportunities
- Stresses its importance in handling peer pressure

CHAPTER 3: A HELPFUL WAY OF THINKING

- Introduces a mindset that supports growth and self-belief
- Examines how thoughts influence feelings and actions
- Teaches methods to handle mistakes in a learning-focused way
- Explores ways to practice healthier self-talk

CHAPTER 4: HANDLING SELF-DOUBT

- Identifies where self-doubt comes from
- Shares techniques to reduce comparison and negative thinking
- Shows how to respond constructively to uncertainty
- Suggests ways to build inner reassurance

CHAPTER 5: COMMUNICATION SKILLS

- Covers clear speaking, active listening, and reading body language
- Explores how confidence grows with better communication

- Offers tips for handling conflicts and misunderstandings
- Provides strategies for group discussions and presentations

CHAPTER 6: BUILDING POSITIVE FRIENDSHIPS

- Discusses spotting healthy versus unhealthy friendship patterns
- Suggests ways to form bonds that support self-esteem
- Explains how respect and trust strengthen relationships
- Covers handling gossip, peer pressure, and jealousy

CHAPTER 7: HANDLING STRESS

- Explains stress causes and how it affects the body and mind
- Outlines coping strategies and relaxation techniques
- Offers ways to find balance with school, family, and hobbies
- Teaches daily habits to reduce overload

CHAPTER 8: BODY IMAGE

- Talks about pressures teens face regarding appearance
- Provides tools to combat negative self-comparison
- Encourages appreciating unique body strengths
- Discusses creating a positive self-view

CHAPTER 9: SETTING AND REACHING GOALS

- Explains why goals give purpose and motivation
- Describes how to create realistic, measurable plans
- Shows how to track progress and stay focused
- Offers advice on overcoming setbacks

CHAPTER 10: HEALTHY RELATIONSHIPS

- Defines core elements like respect, trust, and fairness
- Differentiates between supportive and controlling behaviors
- Discusses family, friendship, and romantic relationship scenarios

- Emphasizes recognizing warning signs of toxic patterns

CHAPTER 11: SOCIAL MEDIA AND SELF-WORTH

- Examines how online comparisons affect confidence
- Suggests responsible social media habits
- Gives tips to stay safe and keep perspective online
- Explains how to handle cyberbullying or negative feedback

CHAPTER 12: OVERCOMING CRITICISM

- Teaches ways to spot useful vs. harmful criticism
- Shows how to respond calmly and take helpful feedback
- Explores turning negative remarks into personal growth
- Includes self-talk and boundary-setting for protection

CHAPTER 13: THE POWER OF POSITIVE ROLE MODELS

- Defines qualities of a good role model
- Suggests ways to learn from others' achievements and mistakes
- Warns of pitfalls in relying on public images alone
- Encourages becoming your own role model over time

CHAPTER 14: TIME MANAGEMENT

- Explores why scheduling reduces stress and boosts self-confidence
- Explains planning methods: daily lists, weekly overviews, priorities
- Advises on avoiding procrastination and burnout
- Connects time management to mental health and success

CHAPTER 15: BOUNDARIES AND RESPECT

- Explains the importance of personal space and emotional safety
- Shows how to communicate boundaries to family and friends
- Offers techniques for handling boundary pushback
- Emphasizes respecting others' lines for healthier relationships

CHAPTER 16: HABITS FOR SELF-CARE

- Covers physical and mental self-care routines
- Suggests small daily habits to lower stress
- Explores creative and social outlets for better balance
- Shows how self-care shapes long-term confidence

CHAPTER 17: FINDING YOUR INTERESTS

- Discusses why exploring hobbies and passions boosts self-esteem
- Explains how to sample clubs, events, and volunteer options
- Guides handling fear of failure and seeking new experiences
- Teaches staying motivated with mini-goals and reflection

CHAPTER 18: DEALING WITH CHANGES

- Talks about physical, emotional, and social shifts in teenage years
- Provides coping methods for moving schools or changing friend groups
- Highlights the power of open-mindedness and flexibility
- Discusses balancing grief over loss with looking forward

CHAPTER 19: SPREADING CONFIDENCE TO OTHERS

- Outlines ways to uplift friends, classmates, and younger teens
- Encourages sharing skills, compliments, and genuine support
- Suggests community involvement and online positivity
- Details handling negativity while staying kind and firm

CHAPTER 20: BUILDING A BRIGHT FUTURE

- Summarizes key lessons for long-term personal growth
- Advises on goal-setting, planning, and adapting to adult roles
- Explores maintaining healthy habits, finances, and relationships
- Encourages continuous learning, resilience, and value-driven living

Chapter 1: Understanding Confidence

1. Introduction

Confidence is a word many people use, but not everyone truly understands. Some people think confidence means acting loud, while others think it means being perfect. In truth, confidence is about being sure of yourself in a steady, balanced way. It does not mean you never feel nervous. It means you believe in who you are, even if you have flaws. This is an important idea for teen girls who are growing and learning every single day.

When you are confident, you can handle different challenges. You can share your thoughts without fear, and you can stand firm when someone disagrees with you. You are also more likely to think positively about your future. Confidence can help you do better in school, make good friends, and feel happier on a daily basis.

Many teen girls wonder why confidence matters so much. After all, is it not enough just to be liked by others? Or to follow what your friends do? The answer is that when you have your own sense of self-worth, you will not rely on outside approval as much. Other people's opinions can still matter, but they will not control you.

This chapter will explain confidence in basic terms. We will look at what confidence is, how it feels, and why it is important to see it as something that grows with time. We will also look at different parts of confidence, such as the role of self-esteem and the impact of your environment. By the end of this chapter, you should have a clear picture of what confidence is and how it applies to your life.

2. What Confidence Really Means

2.1 Defining Confidence

Confidence is a strong belief that you can handle life's situations. It does not mean you think you are the best or that you never make mistakes. It means you have a sense that you can cope, solve problems, and learn from your errors.

Confidence goes hand in hand with self-trust. For example, if you have a big test coming up, you trust that you can study well, manage your time, and do your best. Even if the result is not perfect, you do not lose all faith in yourself. You can step back and think: "What went well? What can I improve?" This kind of attitude helps you grow.

2.2 Confidence vs. Arrogance

Some people mix up confidence with arrogance. Arrogance is when a person acts like they are better than everyone else. Arrogance often comes from insecurity deep down, but it shows up as bragging or putting others down. True confidence does not need to prove anything by belittling other people.

A confident person can say, "I am proud of my skills," while still recognizing other people have their own strengths. A confident person does not feel the need to show off or keep reminding others of their talents. They can stay calm, speak honestly, and treat others with kindness.

2.3 Self-Esteem and Self-Worth

Confidence is also closely tied to self-esteem and self-worth. Self-esteem is how you feel about yourself overall. If you think you are a good person who tries her best, your self-esteem is likely healthy. If you often think, "I am a failure" or "I am not worth anything," your self-esteem may be low.

Self-worth is the basic sense that you have value as a human being. It is about realizing you have something good to offer, just by being you. Even if you struggle in math or do not make the sports team, you can still have a sense of self-worth because you know everyone has something special about them. You do not need to be perfect to be worthy of respect.

These ideas—confidence, self-esteem, and self-worth—connect in many ways. When your self-worth is low, it is harder to feel confident. When you feel confident, you often boost your overall self-esteem because you trust you can do things well. As a teen girl, learning to build these things step by step can help you find stability in who you are.

---

3. Early Influences on Confidence

3.1 Family Environment

Your home life can influence how you see yourself. For example, if your parents or guardians often praise your efforts and support you, you might grow up feeling that your abilities matter. If they encourage you to try new things and do not get overly upset when you fail, you learn that mistakes are not the end of the world. This can give you a stronger sense of confidence later.

On the other hand, if your family is very critical or rarely recognizes your achievements, you might question your abilities. You could start to think you are not capable, even if you do well in some areas. It is important to notice how your family dynamics might shape your view of yourself.

3.2 School Environment

School is a big part of a teen's life. How teachers and classmates treat you can affect your confidence. If teachers encourage class participation and do not shame students who get something wrong, you might feel safer sharing your thoughts. This environment can build your confidence in raising your hand and speaking up.

But if a teacher points out your mistakes in a mean way, you may become scared to participate. Peer groups can also play a huge role. If you have friends who support you, you will feel better about taking on challenges. If you face teasing or bullying, your confidence might drop.

3.3 Social Circles

Outside of school, the friends you spend time with can either lift you up or bring you down. Some friends are understanding. They cheer you on when you try something new or feel nervous. They congratulate you when you succeed in small ways, like finishing a difficult homework assignment.

Other friends might say hurtful comments, even if they claim they are joking. You might feel embarrassed or ashamed. Your self-belief can become shaky if you are surrounded by people who do not appreciate you.

3.4 Media Impact

We live in a world full of social media, TV shows, and movies. The images you see there can set high standards that are hard to reach. You might watch a show where teenagers your age look flawless and always act perfect. You could start comparing yourself to those characters and feel less confident.

Keep in mind that much of media is not real. Pictures are edited and stories are scripted. It is good to remember that real life is different. Knowing this can help you avoid losing confidence from unrealistic comparisons.

---

4. The Feeling of Being Confident

4.1 Emotional Signs

When you feel confident, you may notice a sense of calm. You might still be a bit nervous if you are trying something new, but deep down, you believe you can manage. You may feel lighter and more optimistic about the day ahead. This does not mean you will never have worries, but your worries will not take over.

4.2 Physical Signs

Confidence can also show up in your body language. You might stand up straighter, make eye contact, and speak clearly. When you doubt yourself, you might slouch, speak softly, or avoid looking at people. Training your body to show signs of confidence can also help you feel more confident inside. For instance, simply standing tall or practicing a steady tone of voice can make a difference.

4.3 Mental Clarity

Confidence also has an impact on how you think. When you trust yourself, you tend to have a clearer head. You can weigh options more calmly, rather than falling into panic or negative thoughts. This mental clarity often leads to better decisions. Instead of rushing or avoiding a choice, you think logically and trust your instincts at the same time.

4.4 Effects on Daily Life

Feeling confident can help you in many small ways. For example, you might raise your hand in class more often, which can lead to better understanding of the subject. You may speak to new people without freezing up, making it easier to form friendships. Confidence can also lower stress because you do not worry as much about every mistake or what people think of you.

---

5. Differences Between Confidence, Pride, and Shyness

5.1 Why People Confuse These

Confidence is sometimes mistaken for pride or arrogance. But as we mentioned, confidence does not mean thinking you are the best. It is about self-belief without looking down on others. Pride can become a problem if it leads to refusing to admit mistakes. Arrogance is even more extreme, where a person sees themselves as above everyone else.

Shyness is often misunderstood too. A shy person might be introverted or quiet, but that does not necessarily mean they are not confident. They might simply prefer smaller groups or personal time. You can be shy yet still hold a strong sense of self-worth.

5.2 Healthy Self-Belief

Healthy self-belief means you recognize your strong points and your weak spots. You feel good about what you can do, and you accept where you need to improve. You do not tie your entire worth to being perfect in every area. This balance keeps your confidence real and not forced.

5.3 When Shyness Affects Confidence

Some people become so shy that it stops them from interacting in normal ways. If you always avoid speaking up or trying new things out of fear, it can affect your ability to build confidence. While it is okay to prefer quiet activities or smaller friend groups, it might help to slowly practice being more open. This will remind you that it is safe to share your thoughts and skills with others.

5.4 Breaking Myths

A common myth is that confident people are always outgoing. That is not true. An introverted person can be extremely confident if they trust their abilities and do not let fear rule their decisions. Another myth is that confident people never feel nervous. In reality, confidence is about learning to manage nerves, not magically making them disappear.

6. Common Misunderstandings About Confidence

6.1 You Are Born with Confidence

Some people think certain individuals are just born confident. While personality traits do matter, confidence is also something you build over time through experiences. You gain it by facing challenges, learning new skills, and seeing that you can handle problems. If you are not very confident right now, it does not mean you will never be confident. It just means you may have to put in more effort to develop it.

6.2 Mistakes Destroy Confidence

Another misunderstanding is that making mistakes or failing at something will kill your confidence. This would only be true if you let failure define you. A confident person realizes mistakes are a normal part of learning. In fact, mistakes can sometimes boost your confidence because they teach you how to do better next time.

6.3 Confidence Means No Fear

Fear is a normal emotion. Even the most confident person on stage might have some butterflies in their stomach. The difference is that they do not let fear stop them from acting. They know fear is just an emotion and that it can be managed or lessened. They prepare, practice, and stay focused on what they want to achieve.

6.4 You Need Others to Approve

Some might think confidence only comes from people praising you. While it feels good to get compliments, relying on outside approval for your sense of worth is risky. It means you have to always hope others say good things about you. True confidence means you can appreciate praise but do not require it to feel okay.

7. Steps to Start Building Confidence

7.1 Self-Awareness

The first step in building confidence is becoming aware of what you think about yourself. Pay attention to your inner voice. Do you often say harsh things like, "I cannot do anything right"? Or do you keep your self-talk more balanced, like, "I made a mistake, but I learned something"? Becoming aware of negative thinking can help you change it.

7.2 Setting Small Goals

Confidence grows when you achieve something meaningful to you. Even small tasks can show you that you are capable. For instance, if you are nervous about speaking in class, set a goal to raise your hand once a week. When you do it and realize nothing terrible happens, you build a small win. Over time, small wins add up.

7.3 Practice Positive Talk

A good exercise is to replace negative thoughts with kinder ones. For every negative thought, find one realistic positive thought. For example, if you think, "I will never get better at math," replace it with, "I might struggle now, but I can improve by studying with friends or asking the teacher for help." Doing this repeatedly starts to change how your mind works.

7.4 Learn from Mentors

Look for people who seem confident but are also kind. See how they handle challenges. Talk to a teacher, counselor, or older friend who has gone through what you are facing. Ask them what helped them gain confidence. Their tips might become useful in your own life.

7.5 Track Your Progress

Another helpful habit is to keep a notebook or journal. Write down goals and track your efforts. Also note down what went well. For example, if you gave a short talk in class, jot down how you felt and what you did well. Seeing this written record can remind you of your growth over time.

8. Challenges to Building Confidence

8.1 Fear of Judgment

One of the biggest barriers to confidence is worrying about what others think. This is normal. As a teen, your social world matters a lot. You might worry about being judged if you speak up or try something new. Remember that most people are too busy thinking about their own lives to focus on judging you all the time.

8.2 Past Failures

If you have failed at something major before, you might be scared to try again. But failure is often a teacher. It can show you what not to do. Try to see your past failures as lessons. Ask yourself, "What did I learn from that experience?" This can shift your mindset from shame to growth.

8.3 Lack of Support

Sometimes, you might not have supportive people around you. You might not get encouragement from family or friends. In these cases, it helps to seek out new groups, clubs, or online communities that share your interests. Finding even one person who believes in you can give you the boost you need.

8.4 Comparison with Others

Constantly looking at what others have or do can harm your confidence. You might see a friend who is good at sports and feel bad if you are not as athletic. But everyone has different strengths. Focus on what you enjoy and what skills you can develop. Respect the achievements of others without discounting your own.

9. Practical Exercises to Strengthen Confidence

9.1 Positive Posture Practice

Stand in front of a mirror. Place your feet shoulder-width apart. Lift your head so you are looking straight ahead. Keep your shoulders back but not tense. Breathe slowly. Look at yourself and tell yourself one positive statement. For instance, "I am capable of learning new things." Notice how standing in a stable way can make you feel a bit stronger.

9.2 Guided Visualization

Close your eyes and picture yourself doing something you want to do well in. Maybe it is giving a speech, talking to a new friend, or trying out for a club. Imagine yourself calm, prepared, and doing your best. This mental practice can train your mind to believe you can succeed in real life.

9.3 Role-Playing with a Friend

Ask a trustworthy friend to help you practice a scenario. For example, if you are nervous about a job interview or a school presentation, act it out at home. Have them ask you questions, and then answer as if it is real. This kind of role-play helps you feel more familiar with the situation, lowering anxiety.

9.4 List Your Achievements

Write down things you have achieved, big or small. Maybe you learned a new piece of music, improved your grades in one subject, or cooked a meal for your family. When you see how many things you have done, it can remind you of your capabilities. Place this list somewhere you can see it often.

10. Signs You Are Becoming More Confident

10.1 You Speak Up More Often

One sign of growing confidence is that you do not hold back your thoughts as much. You might find yourself volunteering in class or joining in discussions with friends. Speaking up can still feel a bit scary, but you do it anyway because you trust your thoughts matter.

10.2 You Worry Less About Perfection

Another sign is that you stop chasing perfection. You realize mistakes will happen, but they do not define you. You can laugh off small errors and learn from bigger ones. You understand there is a lot more to life than being perfect.

10.3 You Try New Activities

When you are more confident, you might try things you used to avoid. This could mean joining a new club, learning a musical instrument, or even offering to help a teacher with a project. Your willingness to step into unfamiliar territory grows because you trust yourself to handle what comes.

10.4 You Accept Compliments Gracefully

Some people get very uncomfortable when they receive a compliment. They might say, "It was nothing," or "I got lucky." When your confidence grows, you learn to accept compliments with a simple "Thank you." You feel good about your effort, not in a bragging way, but in a calm, self-assured way.

11. Sustaining Your Confidence Over Time

11.1 Adjusting to Life Changes

Your teen years are full of changes: new schools, new friends, and new responsibilities. Each change can test your confidence. Remember that you can handle more than you think. Think back to times you adapted before. This will remind you that you can manage current changes, too.

11.2 Ongoing Reflection

Confidence is not a one-time achievement. It is something you keep working on. Reflect on your growth once in a while. Think about what is working and what is not. If you notice your confidence slipping, revisit the exercises and steps that helped you before.

11.3 Balancing Humility and Self-Assurance

Staying humble means being open to learning from others. Do not shut down advice or think you know everything. Being confident means you believe in yourself, but also realize there is more to learn. This balance keeps your mindset open and allows continuous growth.

11.4 Celebrating Growth

When you see progress, acknowledge it. This does not mean bragging. You can simply say, "I did better today than last time," or "I am proud I overcame that fear." Giving yourself credit is not a bad thing; it is a healthy way to keep your spirits high.

Chapter 2: Why Confidence Matters for Teen Girls

1. Introduction

In the previous chapter, we explored what confidence is and how it affects you as a person. Now, let us look closer at why it matters so much, especially for teen girls. The teen years are often a time of changes. Your interests might shift, your friendships might change, and you may start to see the world in new ways. While these years can be exciting, they can also be filled with challenges.

During your teen years, you may face more social pressures—like fitting in, looking a certain way, or impressing others. You may also start thinking about your future. With all these pressures, self-belief can play a major role in how you make choices. A strong sense of confidence can be like an anchor, keeping you steady when you face waves of doubt, stress, or confusion.

In this chapter, we will discuss specific reasons why confidence is important for teen girls. We will see how it plays into friendships, academics, and overall mental health. We will also look at some of the common obstacles teen girls face and how a stable sense of self can help you navigate them. By understanding the many ways confidence helps, you can be more motivated to keep working on it.

2. Handling Social Pressure

2.1 Peer Influence

One main reason confidence matters for teen girls is the power of peer pressure. Your friends and classmates can have a strong impact on how you dress, talk, and act. If you are not confident in who you are, you might go along with things that you do not really like or even think are wrong. This might include skipping classes, trying substances, or being mean to someone to fit in.

When you have confidence, you can stand your ground. You are not as likely to be swayed by group pressure. You know what you believe, and even if you feel the pull to conform, you have the strength to say no when it does not match your values.

2.2 Bullying and Teasing

Bullying is another issue teen girls face. This can be verbal (like name-calling), social (like being excluded from a group), or even physical. A bully's words can cut deeply if you already doubt your worth. However, if you have confidence, you are less likely to internalize their harmful comments. You might still feel hurt, but you will not believe every negative thing they say about you.

Confidence can also give you the courage to reach out for help when someone is bullying you. Instead of hiding the problem, you understand that you deserve to be treated with respect, and you seek support from adults or friends.

2.3 Body Image and Beauty Standards

Teen girls often face pressure about how they look. Social media posts and advertisements can set an unrealistic idea of what "beautiful" means. When you are confident, you can separate unrealistic standards from reality. You learn to value your body for its abilities and uniqueness, rather than only focusing on how close it matches someone else's standard.

This does not mean you will never worry about your appearance. But confidence helps you remember that looks are just one part of who you are. You can focus on your talents, kindness, and the many other qualities you have. This broader perspective can prevent destructive behaviors like extreme dieting or harsh self-criticism.

3. Doing Well in School

3.1 Speaking Up in Class

Confidence can help you academically. If you are too nervous to ask questions or share your thoughts, you might miss out on learning. Teachers often appreciate students who show engagement in class, and those who speak up learn more effectively. When you have confidence, you can raise your hand without being terrified of making a mistake. And if you do make a mistake, you accept it as part of the learning process.

3.2 Taking on Challenges

Sometimes you might fear taking a harder class or tackling a big project because you doubt your abilities. Confidence can push you to try these challenges anyway. Even if the class is hard, you believe you have the ability to seek help, study, and improve. This willingness to challenge yourself can lead to better outcomes, not just in grades, but in life skills like problem-solving and perseverance.

3.3 Healthy Competition

Competition can be positive if it motivates you to do your best. But it can become toxic if you only feel good about yourself when you beat others. With confidence, you learn to compete with your past self, aiming to become better each time. You focus on your own growth rather than constantly comparing your results to others. This approach reduces stress and keeps you motivated in a healthier way.

---

4. Boosting Mental Health

4.1 Lowering Stress and Anxiety

A strong sense of self-belief can help lower stress and anxiety. When you trust yourself to handle problems, each challenge feels less threatening.

You might still be concerned about tests or social issues, but you do not spiral into panic as easily. This calmer mindset can help you concentrate on finding solutions instead of getting stuck in worry.

4.2 Decreasing Negative Self-Talk

Negative self-talk is when you speak to yourself in unkind or harsh ways, like saying, "I am worthless" or "I will fail no matter what." Confidence acts as a guard, making it easier to replace those thoughts with more balanced ones. Over time, reducing negative self-talk helps you have a brighter outlook and more emotional stability.

4.3 Building Resilience

Resilience means bouncing back from setbacks. Life will always have ups and downs. Confidence helps you face these downs without losing all hope. If you do badly on an exam or lose a friendship, you still feel sad or disappointed, but you do not see it as the end of the world. You remind yourself you can learn or find new friendships. This ability to recover is a key part of mental wellness.

---

5. Encouraging Healthy Relationships

5.1 Romantic Relationships

During your teen years, you might explore romantic interests. Confidence allows you to set boundaries more clearly. If you are confident, you understand what you are comfortable with and can say so. This lowers the chance of being pressured into situations you do not want. It also helps you pick partners who respect you, rather than settling for someone who treats you poorly because you feel you cannot do any better.

5.2 Friendships

Confidence can improve your friendships too. When you feel good about yourself, you are less likely to depend on your friends to constantly make you feel worthy. You can support them without losing yourself. Also, you can recognize unhealthy friendship patterns—like a friend who always puts you down—and either address it or walk away if needed.

5.3 Family Connections

Sometimes teen girls have conflicts with parents, siblings, or other relatives. While disagreements are normal, confidence helps you discuss problems in a calm manner. You can express what you feel or need without shouting or letting anger take over. This open communication can lead to stronger family bonds.

---

6. Decision-Making and Independence

6.1 Trusting Your Own Judgment

Teen years often bring bigger decisions, like choosing elective classes, managing free time, or deciding on future career paths. Confidence helps you trust your instincts. Even if you seek advice from others, you do not rely on them to make your choices. You weigh their opinions, think about what feels right for you, and then decide.

6.2 Avoiding Harmful Activities

Peer pressure can sometimes push teens into risky behaviors. A confident teen girl is more likely to say no to activities that go against her values or harm her well-being. This includes anything from skipping school to trying substances. Confidence does not mean you never feel tempted, but it gives you the strength to stand by what is safe and right for you.

6.3 Preparing for the Future

Thinking about college or careers can be overwhelming. A confident approach can help you research your options, talk to counselors, and try out internships or volunteer work. You believe you can learn new skills, adapt to new situations, and keep growing. This mindset is crucial as you step into adulthood.

7. Avoiding the Pitfalls of Low Confidence

7.1 Self-Isolation

Without confidence, some teen girls might pull back from others. They might fear rejection or judgment so much that they avoid social events, clubs, or even group projects. This isolation can feed into loneliness and further lower self-esteem. It becomes a cycle that is hard to break. Recognizing this trap is a first step to fighting it.

7.2 Settling for Less

Low confidence can cause someone to settle for less than they deserve. Whether it is in friendships, romantic relationships, or school performance, they might think they cannot do any better. They stay in bad friendships or do not apply for that leadership role because they do not believe in themselves. Over time, this can lead to regret and a sense of missed opportunities.

7.3 Overdependence on Approval

If your confidence is low, you might constantly seek approval from others—friends, family, or even strangers on social media. Each like or comment can feel like a small boost, but it does not last. You may then feel anxious when the approval is not there. A healthier approach is knowing how to encourage yourself, so you are not relying solely on outside validation.

8. Positive Outcomes of Confidence

8.1 Better Communication

When teen girls have confidence, they communicate more clearly. They speak up about their needs and ask questions when they are unsure. This skill can lead to fewer misunderstandings, better teamwork on school projects, and stronger friendships built on honest communication.

8.2 Ability to Lead

Confidence can turn you into a leader, even in small ways. You might not become the class president, but you could lead a study group or organize a community service event. People are drawn to someone who seems secure and fair-minded. Being a leader can further boost your confidence because you see that others trust you.

8.3 Growth Mindset

Confidence feeds a growth mindset, which means you believe you can develop your talents through effort. With this outlook, you do not see failures as final. You see them as moments to learn. This helps you become more creative and open to trying new things. Over time, this approach can open doors you never expected.

---

9. Real-Life Scenarios

9.1 Standing Against Peer Pressure

Imagine you are at a party and people you know start doing something risky. They might challenge you to join. If you have low confidence, you might agree just to avoid being left out, even if you are scared. If you are confident, you calmly say no and stick to it. Sure, it might be awkward, but you protect yourself and stay true to what you believe.

9.2 Handling a Class Presentation

Let's say you need to give a presentation to your class. With low confidence, you might dread it and consider calling in sick. If you do go through with it, you might speak very softly, rush through your words, or avoid eye contact. With confidence, you might still feel nervous, but you prepare well and tell yourself you can do it. Even if you stumble on a word, you keep going. When it is over, you feel a sense of achievement.

9.3 Responding to Online Comments

Many teen girls experience negative comments on social media. A single rude remark might make you feel awful about yourself if you rely heavily on outside approval. With confidence, you can recognize that one post does not define you. You might block or ignore the person, or respond politely if it seems appropriate. You move on rather than obsessing over it.

---

10. Overcoming Obstacles to Confidence

10.1 Finding Support Systems

One key to fighting doubt is to find supportive friends or mentors. These are people who like you for who you are and cheer you on when you try something new. They also respect your boundaries. If your current circle does not give you that, look for different groups—clubs at school or online communities dedicated to healthy interests.

10.2 Counseling or Guidance

Sometimes you might benefit from talking to a counselor or a trusted adult. If you are dealing with deep-rooted self-esteem issues, a professional can guide you through strategies to build yourself up. They can help you sort out past hurt, such as bullying experiences, that might still affect how you see yourself.

10.3 Trying New Activities

An effective way to build confidence is to try something unfamiliar. Whether it is a new sport, a coding club, or an art class, stepping outside your comfort zone can show you strengths you did not know you had. Even if you do not excel right away, you learn you are capable of taking on new challenges.

10.4 Setting Realistic Goals

Sometimes teen girls set extremely high goals, like getting perfect grades in every class while also being the star of a sports team, and so on. When those goals are not met, they feel like failures. Setting realistic goals helps you taste success and grow your confidence gradually. You can always aim higher later.

---

11. Building Confidence in Daily Life

11.1 Daily Affirmations

Each morning, you can say a short statement to yourself that is positive. For example: "I am strong," "I learn from mistakes," or "I have value." While this might feel odd at first, repeating supportive words can slowly shift your mindset. Over time, your brain starts to adopt these messages as truths.

11.2 Tracking Moments of Courage

Use a small notebook or an app on your phone to note when you show courage in daily life. Maybe you helped a new student find their way, or you spoke your mind in a debate. These small wins build a larger sense of self-belief. Reading through them later can remind you of how far you have come.

11.3 Physical Health

Confidence is also connected to how you feel physically. Getting enough sleep, eating well, and exercising in a way you enjoy can boost your mood and energy. When you feel better in your body, you often feel better in your mind. This does not mean you must meet a certain beauty standard. Rather, it is about taking basic care of yourself to maintain your well-being.

11.4 Sharing Positivity

Sometimes, being kind to someone else can improve your own sense of self-worth. Offering genuine compliments, helping a friend study, or volunteering in the community gives you a sense of purpose. You realize you can make a difference, which boosts your belief in yourself.

---

12. Long-Term Benefits

12.1 Stronger Adult Life

Confidence you build now can carry over into your adult life. It can help you handle job interviews, form healthy relationships, and face unexpected life problems. Starting early to build self-belief gives you a head start in becoming a well-adjusted adult who can cope with the stress of the real world.

12.2 Positive Influence on Others

When you show confidence without putting others down, you become a role model. Younger girls or even peers might look to you as someone who knows her worth. Your behavior can spread the message that it is okay to stand up for yourself and that you do not have to follow every trend just to fit in.

12.3 Greater Sense of Fulfillment

Feeling confident allows you to explore your interests and passions without being weighed down by too much self-doubt. You give yourself permission to dream and try new paths. Whether you want to become a writer, a scientist, a teacher, or an artist, confidence helps you take the steps needed to get there.

---

13. Challenges Unique to Teen Girls

13.1 Cultural Expectations

In some places, girls might face expectations on how they should behave, speak, or dress. These rules can be strict and might limit a girl's sense of freedom. Confidence is especially important in challenging these limits, where you learn to make decisions that feel right for you while still respecting certain cultural values that do not harm you.

13.2 Balancing Activities

Teen girls often juggle multiple roles—being a student, a daughter, a friend, and maybe a part-time worker or club leader. Confidence can help you set boundaries so you do not burn out. It also aids you in communicating when you need help. This balanced approach ensures you do not take on more than you can manage.

13.3 Dealing with Stereotypes

Society sometimes promotes stereotypes, such as telling girls they are not good at math or they should not be too outspoken. A confident girl can question these stereotypes. She can prove that girls are strong, smart, and capable of leading. This attitude can inspire change not just in her own life, but in how others see teen girls as well.

14. Ways Parents and Guardians Can Help

14.1 Positive Feedback

Parents can play a big role in encouraging confidence. For example, when a parent notices their daughter studied hard or showed kindness to someone, they can offer specific praise about that action. Hearing "You are kind for helping that person today" can reinforce the idea that you have good qualities to be proud of.

14.2 Allowing Independence

While it is natural for parents to worry, giving a teen girl some space to make her own decisions can help her build confidence. This might involve letting her choose her own hobbies or manage her allowance. Feeling trusted is a big part of feeling capable.

14.3 Setting a Good Example

Parents who speak positively about themselves and others show their children how to have a healthy mindset. If a mother or father always criticizes their own appearance or abilities, a teen girl might pick up the habit of negative self-talk. Conversely, seeing a parent handle failure calmly can teach a daughter that mistakes are not the end of the world.

Chapter 4: Handling Self-Doubt

1. Introduction

Everyone experiences self-doubt at some point. It can show up when you are about to speak in front of a group, try out for a team, or even talk to someone you like. Self-doubt is that inner voice that asks, "Are you sure you can do this?" or states, "You might fail. Maybe you should back out." While a bit of doubt can be normal, too much of it can block you from exploring your abilities or enjoying life.

In this chapter, we will look at where self-doubt comes from, how it differs from healthy caution, and what you can do to keep it from running your life. You will learn to spot the signals of self-doubt, handle negative feedback, and replace harmful inner messages with more constructive ones. By the end, you should feel more able to manage self-doubt so that it no longer holds you back from what you want to do.

2. The Roots of Self-Doubt

2.1 Early Life Influences

Sometimes self-doubt starts in childhood. If parents, teachers, or other adults were overly critical or rarely praised your efforts, you might have grown up believing you were not capable. Even small statements—like constantly being compared to a sibling or being scolded for minor mistakes—can plant seeds of doubt. Over time, those seeds can grow into a persistent feeling that you are never quite good enough.

2.2 Past Failures

Another source of self-doubt is previous experiences of failure. If you once tried out for the school play and forgot your lines on stage, you might now worry every time you have to speak publicly. Your brain remembers that embarrassing moment and tries to protect you from feeling that way again. While it is a normal response, it can become too strong, stopping you from giving future attempts a fair shot.

2.3 Fear of Judgment

Many teens worry about what others think. Whether it is your friends, classmates, or people online, the fear of being laughed at or criticized can create a strong sense of self-doubt. This is made worse by social media, where it can feel like everyone is watching what you post or do. In reality, people are often more focused on themselves than on judging you. But when you do not realize that, it can feed constant worry.

2.4 Unrealistic Expectations

If you hold yourself to an extremely high standard—like thinking you must always score the highest in class or never make a social slip-up—you set yourself up for doubt. The second you see anything less than perfect, you feel like a failure. This pressure can come from within or from external factors, like parents who expect top grades in every subject. Over time, these standards make you doubt any success that is not "flawless."

---

3. Self-Doubt vs. Humility

3.1 Healthy Caution

It is important to note that self-doubt is not always bad. Sometimes it serves as a check to make you practice more or think carefully about an action. For example, if you doubt your ability to run a marathon without any training, that doubt might be healthy. It reminds you that you need preparation or guidance.

3.2 Differentiating Between the Two

- **Humility:** Recognizing that you have more to learn. Staying open to advice. A humble person might say, "I want to do well, but I know I need to study and put in the work."
- **Paralyzing Self-Doubt:** Believing you cannot learn or improve, to the point where you do not even try. You might say, "There is no use even starting because I will fail for sure."

Being humble allows room for growth. Paralyzing self-doubt shuts down your willingness to move forward.

---

4. Signs That Self-Doubt Is Holding You Back

4.1 You Avoid Trying New Things

A major indicator of self-doubt is constantly saying "no" to new chances. You might think, "I will probably fail, so why bother?" This pattern can stop you from discovering activities or skills you could actually enjoy or be good at.

4.2 You Seek Constant Assurance

It is normal to want some support from others. But if you find yourself unable to make any decision—big or small—without someone else's approval, your self-doubt might be too strong. This can include texting friends non-stop to see if an outfit is okay or asking your parents to solve every minor problem for you.

4.3 You Downplay Your Achievements

When you do something well, do you brush it off as luck or say it was "no big deal"? Constantly downplaying your own success can be a sign you do not believe you deserve credit or praise. This attitude can stop you from recognizing your real strengths.

4.4 You Worry Excessively About Judgment

While some concern about others' opinions is normal, self-doubt can magnify it. You might spend hours analyzing someone's facial expression, wondering if they secretly think you are annoying or incompetent. This level of overthinking can cause high stress and lower your confidence.

---

5. Breaking Down Self-Doubt Step by Step

5.1 Step 1: Recognize Your Doubt Triggers

Start by identifying the situations or people that make your self-doubt flare up. Is it speaking in public? Is it a certain friend who is very critical? Pinpointing triggers helps you know when to apply coping techniques.

5.2 Step 2: Question the Doubt

When a doubtful thought arises, ask yourself: "Is this fact or just my fear talking?" Often, you might find that it is fear, not truth. For instance, "I will mess up this speech for sure" is not a proven fact. It is a prediction your mind makes to protect you from risk. But you have no real evidence that you will definitely mess up.

5.3 Step 3: Gather Evidence of Success

Look at your past. Perhaps you did speak in public once and it went okay, or you did better than expected. Maybe you got positive feedback from a teacher on an essay you thought was not great. Listing your successes—even small ones—can act like a shield against self-doubt.

5.4 Step 4: Take Safe Risks

Start with small steps that stretch your comfort zone but are not overwhelming. If you fear social gatherings, maybe join a small study group before going to a big party. If you are unsure about your art skills, show your drawings to one trusted friend before trying to display them publicly. Each small success helps reduce self-doubt a bit more.

---

6. Techniques to Handle Negative Feedback

6.1 Evaluating the Source

Not all feedback is helpful. If a random person online criticizes you, it might not hold the same weight as feedback from a teacher who knows your work or a coach who has seen your progress. Learn to identify whether the person giving feedback has real insight or if they are simply attacking you without reason.

6.2 Finding the Helpful Part

Even negative feedback can contain something useful. For example, if your teacher notes that your writing lacks clear topic sentences, that is something you can fix. Focus on the part that you can act on, rather than the emotional sting.

6.3 Setting Boundaries

Sometimes the best way to handle overly harsh feedback is to step away. If certain social media groups or peers only make you feel worse about yourself, consider muting or avoiding them. Protecting your mental space is a key part of building confidence.

---

7. Building Trust in Your Abilities

7.1 Self-Trust Through Practice

One reason self-doubt thrives is a lack of experience. If you never speak up in class, you do not get a chance to see that you can do it successfully. Try practicing skills you doubt in small, manageable ways. Repetition builds familiarity, and familiarity can reduce fear.

7.2 Celebrating Progress

Just like in the previous chapter, taking note of small wins can reinforce self-trust. For instance, if you manage to answer one question confidently in class, write it down. Recognizing these moments, however tiny, can shift your mindset from "I cannot" to "Maybe I can."

7.3 Imagining the Outcome

Picture yourself handling a challenge well. If it is a school presentation, see yourself speaking calmly, remembering your points, and finishing strong. This kind of mental picture can cut down on the negative images your self-doubt creates. When your mind can visualize success, you may feel a bit more ready to try.

---

8. Changing the Story You Tell Yourself

8.1 The Power of Personal Narratives

We all have stories about who we are, like, "I am the quiet one," "I am not a leader," or "I always mess up under pressure." These labels can become self-fulfilling. If you believe you always mess up, you might not prepare or you might panic, making mistakes more likely. Changing your personal narrative starts with recognizing those labels and challenging them.

8.2 Finding a New Label

Try to replace harmful labels with more flexible ones. If you always say, "I am just not a math person," switch to, "I can improve in math with extra help and practice." If you call yourself "shy," try saying, "I prefer smaller groups, but I can still voice my opinion." These changes might sound small, but they shift your identity from something fixed to something that can grow.

8.3 Telling the Story of Your Resilience

Look back at tough times you overcame. Maybe you had a bad argument with a friend but then managed to make peace. Maybe you failed a test once but later improved. These stories show you have faced challenges before and managed somehow. Remind yourself of these when self-doubt tries to convince you that you cannot handle anything difficult.

---

9. Addressing Self-Doubt in Specific Areas

9.1 Academic Self-Doubt

- **Tip 1:** If you think you are not smart enough, check your study habits. Could you improve your routine or seek help from classmates or teachers? Often, it is not about IQ but about finding the right study strategies.
- **Tip 2:** Join study groups. Explaining topics to peers can boost your own confidence in the material.

9.2 Social Self-Doubt

- **Tip 1:** Practice small talk in settings where the stakes are low, like chatting briefly with a friendly classmate.
- **Tip 2:** Remember, most people are busy thinking about their own worries. They are not analyzing your every move.

9.3 Self-Doubt in Activities (Sports, Arts, etc.)

- **Tip 1:** Break down skills into smaller pieces. If you want to get better at basketball, maybe start by practicing your dribbling for 15 minutes each day.
- **Tip 2:** Track little improvements. Overcoming self-doubt in sports or arts often requires seeing small increments of progress, like scoring one extra basket than you did before or learning one new chord on the guitar.

10. The Role of Mentors and Supportive Peers

10.1 Finding the Right Guidance

A good mentor or supportive peer can help spot your potential when you cannot see it. They might suggest resources, techniques, or small goals you have not considered. For example, a teacher might notice you have a knack for writing even if you do not believe it. Listening to someone who has your best interests at heart can help counter your self-doubt.

10.2 Open Communication

Share your doubts with a trusted adult or friend. Sometimes just saying it out loud helps reduce its power. You might feel silly confessing, "I am scared no one will like my work," but talking it through can reveal that your worry is bigger in your head than in reality.

10.3 Group Accountability

If you are working on a project or skill, teaming up with friends who have similar goals can keep you motivated. You cheer each other on, share setbacks, and celebrate improvements. This communal support can help reduce the isolating feeling self-doubt often brings.

---

11. Handling Criticism and Failure as Fuel for Growth

11.1 Rewriting the Meaning of Failure

What if, instead of seeing failure as a final statement on your worth, you saw it as data? If you do poorly on a test, that does not mean you are dumb. It might mean your study method was not effective, or you need to review the material longer. Re-labeling failure as information on what to adjust next time helps you move forward instead of getting stuck in self-blame.

11.2 Learning to Adapt

Many successful people talk about how they failed multiple times before succeeding. The difference is they adapted. They changed strategies, sought new advice, or put in more hours. Self-doubt tries to stop you from trying again. A growth-focused view encourages you to adapt and keep going.

11.3 Turning Criticism into Steps

When someone criticizes you, ask, "What can I learn from this?" Maybe your coach says your footwork is weak. Instead of feeling worthless, direct your energy to practicing footwork drills. Taking action transforms criticism into growth, minimizing the voice of self-doubt that says, "You will never get better."

---

12. Combating Negative Self-Comparison

12.1 The Comparison Trap

It is tempting to compare yourself to classmates, celebrities, or social media influencers. However, comparisons often ignore context. You see someone's highlight reel but not the struggle behind the scenes. This can create the false idea that everyone else is perfect while you are the only one with flaws.

12.2 Focusing on Your Own Path

Instead of tracking how you measure up to others, track your own progress. Are you better at an activity today than you were a month ago? Did you learn something new this week that you did not know before? These personal milestones matter more than how someone else is doing.

12.3 Limiting Social Media Exposure

If scrolling through posts makes you feel inferior, limit that time. Remind yourself that most people only show polished versions of their lives online. Real life is messy for everyone. Reducing the time you spend comparing your everyday reality to someone's "perfect" highlights can lower self-doubt.

---

13. Creating a Self-Doubt "Emergency Kit"

13.1 Why an Emergency Kit?

Self-doubt can strike at random times—maybe right before you go on stage or just as you are about to submit an important assignment. Having an "emergency kit" of strategies can help you handle that panic quickly.

13.2 Items in the Kit

1. **A Quick Positive Note:** Keep a small note in your wallet or phone with a brief encouraging sentence. Something like, "I have succeeded before, I can do it again."
2. **Relaxation Technique:** This could be a deep breathing exercise or a short mindful moment you have practiced.
3. **List of Achievements:** Write down a few achievements or good qualities you have. Reading them can remind you of your capabilities.
4. **Music or Media That Calms You:** A favorite song or relaxing audio can help ground you and distract your mind from spiraling into doubt.

13.3 Testing the Kit

Try using these tools in less stressful situations first, so you know how they work. That way, when a high-pressure moment comes, you will be ready and familiar with your go-to strategies.

14. Self-Doubt and Professional Help

14.1 Knowing When to Seek Extra Support

If your self-doubt is leading to panic attacks, severe avoidance behaviors, or deep sadness, it might be time to talk to a counselor or therapist. Professionals can provide tailored methods to address persistent self-doubt and can help you work through underlying issues that might be driving it.

14.2 Therapy Options

- **Cognitive Behavioral Therapy (CBT):** Helps you spot negative thought patterns and replace them with healthier ones.
- **Talk Therapy:** Allows you to discuss your worries in a safe space and get feedback from a trained individual.
- **Group Therapy:** Lets you meet others dealing with similar issues, showing you that you are not alone.

14.3 Speaking to a School Counselor

Most schools have guidance counselors who can provide support or direct you to outside resources. If you find it hard to bring up your self-doubt with friends or family, a school counselor can be a confidential ear. They can also help you manage academic stress if that is fueling your doubt.

15. A Vision for Life Beyond Self-Doubt

15.1 What Changes When You Conquer Doubt

When you learn to keep self-doubt in check, you open up new possibilities. You might volunteer for leadership roles you used to shrink from. You may feel more relaxed in social settings. You might notice that everyday stressors no longer weigh on you as heavily.

15.2 Realistic Expectations

Conquering self-doubt does not mean you will never feel uncertain again. You will. Everyone does at times. The difference is that it will not stop you from moving forward. You will have strategies to handle that uncertainty rather than letting it control your actions or define your worth.

15.3 Ongoing Maintenance

Dealing with self-doubt is like taking care of a garden. You cannot just plant seeds once and forget about them. You have to water them, remove weeds, and give them sunlight regularly. In the same way, you will need to keep practicing positive self-talk, setting healthy goals, and seeking support when you need it. These habits keep the "weeds" of self-doubt from taking over again.

Chapter 5: Communication Skills

1. Introduction

Communication is how we share ideas, thoughts, and feelings with other people. We use words when we talk, we use our faces and bodies when we show emotions, and we write messages to express more detailed ideas. As a teen girl who wants to build confidence, good communication skills are powerful tools. When you can clearly share what you mean, you reduce misunderstandings, form closer connections, and feel more sure of yourself.

Many people think talking is the only part of communication. But listening, understanding body language, and choosing the right words all matter just as much. Also, in today's world, online messages play a bigger role than ever. Whether you are chatting with friends on social media or sending an email to a teacher, you need to be mindful of what you say and how you say it.

This chapter will explain the different parts of communication so you can see why they are useful. You will learn about listening with care, speaking in a clear manner, and reading nonverbal cues like posture and expressions. We will also look at how to handle disagreements respectfully and ways to avoid common pitfalls, such as talking over someone. By the end, you should have a better grasp of how to use communication skills to boost your confidence and improve your relationships.

---

2. Why Communication Skills Matter for Teen Girls

Communication influences many areas of your life. Whether you are talking with your parents about weekend plans, working on a group project in school, or texting a friend about a problem, how you speak and listen can change the outcome. When your words are thoughtful, people are more likely to understand you. Likewise, when you can listen well, you are more likely to see the other person's point of view.

As a teen girl, you may face special pressures. You might want to blend in with your friends while also wanting to be genuine. You might worry about being judged for your opinions. Communication skills help with these stresses in many ways:

1. **Reduces Conflict:** If a misunderstanding happens among friends, clear communication can clear things up quickly.
2. **Builds Respect:** When you speak calmly and also listen, others see you as fair and strong.
3. **Promotes Self-Assurance:** Every time you stand up for yourself with clear words, you strengthen your self-belief.
4. **Opens Opportunities:** Good communication can help you do better in class discussions or extracurricular activities. Teachers, coaches, and friends can see that you bring ideas to the table.

In short, learning how to communicate well can make your teen years smoother, as you will be better equipped to deal with various challenges. Over time, these skills also prepare you for adulthood, where you may face job interviews, deeper friendships, and more complex family matters.

3. Different Forms of Communication

Communication can happen in several ways, and each way has its own strengths and challenges. Understanding these different forms can help you adapt based on your situation:

1. **Verbal Communication:** This is when you use words out loud. It includes the tone of your voice, how fast or slow you speak, and even the pauses you take.
2. **Nonverbal Communication:** This includes gestures, facial expressions, posture, and eye contact. Sometimes, nonverbal signals can say more than words.

3. **Written Communication:** Writing emails, text messages, and social media posts are all types of written communication. Word choice, spelling, punctuation, and how you organize sentences matter here.

A confident communicator pays attention to all three forms. You may be good at talking but struggle to catch subtle facial expressions. Or you might write well but find it hard to speak in a group. Identifying these gaps is the first step toward improvement. Over time, you can grow more comfortable with each form of communication.

4. Active Listening and Why It Matters

4.1 Understanding Active Listening

Active listening is more than just hearing words. It is about paying close attention, showing the speaker you care, and making an effort to understand. When you practice active listening, you might nod or add small phrases like, "I see" or "Yes, that makes sense," to let the other person know you are following along. You might also ask questions if you are unsure about something they said.

4.2 How Active Listening Builds Confidence

- **Shows Respect:** By listening deeply, you signal that the person's thoughts matter, which often makes them more open to hearing your views too.
- **Reduces Misunderstandings:** When you listen closely, you catch important details and avoid confusion. This can help you respond well, boosting your self-confidence.
- **Improves Relationships:** People trust and appreciate someone who listens to them. This trust can make you feel more valued, which can raise your self-esteem.

4.3 Tips for Better Listening

1. **Face the Speaker:** Turn your body and eyes toward the person talking.
2. **Put Away Distractions:** If you are scrolling on your phone or looking around the room, you will miss key points.
3. **Hold Back Immediate Reactions:** Instead of planning your reply while the other person is still talking, let them finish.
4. **Reflect:** Once they finish, restate what you heard to ensure you got it right.

Active listening might feel a bit awkward at first, especially if you are used to chatting quickly or multi-tasking. But practicing it can bring immediate improvements in how people respond to you. Over time, you will see that truly hearing others also helps you feel more confident about sharing your own ideas.

---

5. Speaking Clearly: Tone, Volume, and Word Choice

5.1 Importance of Tone

Tone is the emotional color of your voice. Sometimes we say one thing, but our tone suggests something else. For instance, if you say "I'm fine" in a shaky, quiet voice, it might show you are not fine at all. Being aware of your tone helps you communicate what you really mean. A confident tone usually sounds steady, without being too loud or too soft.

5.2 Volume Control

Speaking too softly can make it hard for people to hear you, suggesting you are unsure. Speaking too loudly can sound aggressive. Finding the right volume depends on the setting. In a crowded, noisy space, you may need to raise your voice a bit. In a quiet room, a moderate volume is best.

5.3 Choosing Words Wisely

- **Clarity:** Use words that clearly say what you mean. Avoid unnecessary jargon or slang if you are trying to make a serious point.
- **Conciseness:** Sometimes, fewer words can be more powerful, especially when you want to stress a key idea.
- **Positivity:** Try not to load your sentences with negative phrases, especially when talking about yourself. For example, say "I need more practice" instead of "I'm terrible at this."

5.4 Practice for Improvement

Practice speaking in front of a mirror or record yourself on your phone. Notice if your voice sounds shaky or if you talk too fast when you are nervous. By doing short recordings, you can spot areas to work on, like pausing more often or raising your voice slightly when you are about to make a key point. Over time, you will gain a steadier, calmer voice that reflects your growing self-assurance.

---

6. Body Language and Facial Expressions

6.1 Why Nonverbal Cues Are Important

Nonverbal communication can sometimes matter more than spoken words. If someone slouches with folded arms, even if they say they are "open to ideas," their body suggests the opposite. Similarly, if you avoid eye contact, others might think you are insecure or not being genuine. Learning to read and send nonverbal cues can help you feel more confident and aware during conversations.

6.2 Key Body Language Tips

1. **Posture:** Stand or sit up straight, with your shoulders relaxed. This shows that you are alert and at ease.

2. **Eye Contact:** Looking at someone's eyes (without staring too intensely) shows respect and focus. If looking directly in the eyes is uncomfortable, try looking at the space between their eyes.
3. **Facial Expressions:** A gentle smile or a concerned look can show empathy or understanding. Pay attention to tension in your jaw or forehead, which might indicate stress.
4. **Hand Gestures:** Natural hand gestures can help underline your points. But be careful not to wave your hands too much, as it can distract from what you are saying.

6.3 Watching Others

One way to improve your own nonverbal cues is to observe others. Notice how confident speakers stand, or how good listeners nod or lean in. Observe how a friend's face changes when they talk about something exciting versus something sad. This awareness helps you understand what signals you might be sending yourself. Over time, you can adjust your body language so that it supports your words, adding to your overall confidence.

---

7. Handling Disagreements and Conflict

7.1 The Purpose of Conflict

Conflict is a natural part of life. People have different opinions, wants, and beliefs. Learning to manage conflict calmly helps you maintain healthy relationships and keeps small problems from growing bigger. Feeling confident in these moments can be challenging, but the right approaches can reduce stress.

7.2 Tips for Productive Disagreement

1. **Stay Calm:** If you feel your heart racing or your voice shaking, take a slow breath. Pausing for a moment can prevent you from saying something in anger.

2. **Use "I" Statements:** Instead of saying "You always ignore me," try "I feel ignored when you do not respond to my texts." This way, you talk about how you feel without blaming.
3. **Listen to Understand:** Even if you disagree, let the other person explain their position. This makes them more likely to listen to yours.
4. **Seek Solutions Together:** After both sides share their points, think about ways to fix the situation. Maybe you can compromise, or maybe you just need clearer rules about how you will communicate next time.

7.3 Knowing When to Walk Away

Sometimes, the other person might not be ready to solve the conflict calmly. If things are getting heated or unsafe, it is okay to step back and suggest talking later. Walking away does not mean you lost. It can show that you respect yourself enough not to stay in a harmful situation. Once both sides have cooled down, you can come back with a clearer mind.

---

8. Communication in Group Settings

8.1 Challenges in Groups

Group discussions, such as school projects or club meetings, can be stressful. With multiple people trying to speak, it is easy to feel overlooked. You might worry your ideas are not as good, or you might get lost if the conversation moves too quickly. Learning how to speak up in a group is a valuable skill that can boost your confidence and leadership abilities.

8.2 Strategies for Contributing

1. **Prepare Ahead:** If you know the topic, jot down key points you would like to share. This helps you feel ready.
2. **Speak Early:** If you wait too long, you might get more nervous. Insert a quick comment early on, even if it is a simple agreement with someone else's point.

3. **Ask Questions:** If you are not sure when to jump in, ask a clarifying question. This shows you are listening and might open a space for your ideas.
4. **Stay Organized:** Keep track of who has spoken and what they have said. If you can connect your point to something said earlier, it shows you are paying attention.

8.3 Taking Leadership Roles

If you want to build confidence, try offering to lead a small part of a group discussion. For example, you might volunteer to keep track of time or summarize the main ideas. These tasks may seem small, but they can improve your standing in the group and show you are committed. Over time, you might feel comfortable taking on bigger leadership roles, such as being the spokesperson or the organizer.

---

9. Online Communication and Social Media

9.1 The Double-Edged Nature of Online Messages

Texting and social media are quick and easy ways to communicate, but they can also create misunderstandings. Without the tone of voice or body language, a simple text might be read in the wrong way. Plus, online anonymity can lead some people to be ruder than they would be in person. As a teen girl trying to boost confidence, you need to be mindful of how you handle online interactions.

9.2 Tips for Healthy Online Chats

1. **Think Before You Post:** Once you write something online, it is hard to take it back. Ask yourself if this post or comment is helpful, kind, or necessary.
2. **Avoid Over-Sharing:** Personal details about yourself or others do not always belong in the public eye. Protect your safety by keeping sensitive information private.

3. **Use a Clear Tone:** Since people cannot hear your voice, pick words that clearly show what you mean. If you are joking, maybe add a friendly emoji.
4. **Don't Assume Intent:** If a friend's text seems harsh, they might just be busy or stressed. Ask politely for clarity instead of jumping to conclusions.

9.3 Handling Online Conflict

Conflicts can occur online too, especially through group chats or social media threads. The same rules of calm communication apply. Try to take the conversation to a private message if possible, or suggest talking in person. Remember, online arguments can quickly escalate if multiple people join in or misinterpret comments. Keeping your cool can safeguard your self-confidence and your friendships.

---

10. Asking for Help and Setting Boundaries

10.1 Why Asking for Help Is Good

It takes courage to admit you need help, whether it is with schoolwork, a personal problem, or a tough decision. Asking a teacher for extra practice, seeking advice from a friend, or talking to a counselor is a form of communication that shows you respect your own well-being. This can actually increase your sense of self-worth because it proves you are taking action to improve.

10.2 How to Ask for Help Properly

1. **Be Specific:** If you need help in math, do not just say, "I don't get any of this." Try, "I'm having trouble understanding how to solve quadratic equations."
2. **Show Willingness to Learn:** Let the person know you have tried your best so far. For example, "I watched tutorial videos, but I still can't solve these problems."

3. **Thank the Person:** Show gratitude for their time or input. A simple "Thanks for explaining this" or "I appreciate your support" can go a long way.

10.3 Setting Personal Boundaries

Just as you should be free to ask for help, you also have the right to say no when a situation makes you uncomfortable. Maybe a friend asks to copy your homework, or a person online keeps asking personal questions. Clear communication about your limits can protect your sense of safety and self-respect. For instance, you can say, "I'm sorry, but I'm not okay with sharing my answers." Asserting your boundaries in a calm and firm manner can reinforce your confidence because it reminds you that your comfort and values matter.

---

11. Dealing with Criticism Through Words

11.1 Understanding Criticism

Criticism is a form of feedback that points out what might be wrong or could be improved. Some criticism is helpful, like a teacher telling you how to improve an essay. Some criticism is hurtful, especially if delivered with insults or mean comments. As a teen, you might get both types from various sources—family, friends, and even strangers online.

11.2 Receiving Helpful Criticism

1. **Listen Calmly:** Even if it stings, try not to interrupt the person right away.
2. **Ask Questions:** If you are confused about their points, ask for more details.
3. **Thank Them if Appropriate:** For constructive tips, a brief "Thank you for letting me know" can show you appreciate their input.
4. **Decide What to Use:** After hearing the criticism, choose what is valid and what might not apply. You do not have to change everything someone else thinks you should.

11.3 Handling Hurtful Criticism

If someone insults you rather than giving constructive tips, you can stand up for yourself in a calm voice: "I understand you don't like my project, but please give me specific reasons so I can improve." If the person just wants to hurt your feelings, it may be best to walk away or end the conversation. You do not owe anyone your time if they are not respecting you. This type of boundary-setting is a form of communication that shows self-respect.

---

12. Building Empathy in Communication

12.1 What Is Empathy?

Empathy is the ability to understand and share someone else's feelings. It does not mean you agree with them about everything, but rather that you can imagine how they might feel in their situation. Empathy can make your communication more genuine and caring.

12.2 Using Empathy to Communicate Better

1. **Ask How They Feel:** Sometimes, people talk about what happened without saying how it affects them. Asking, "How did that make you feel?" shows concern.
2. **Listen for Hidden Emotions:** Maybe your friend sounds angry, but they are actually hurt. By noticing small changes in their tone or expressions, you can respond more kindly.
3. **Validate Their Feelings:** You might say, "That sounds really upsetting," or "I can see why you are worried about this." Validation does not mean you have to fix the problem. It means you recognize their emotions are real.

12.3 Benefits for Your Own Confidence

When you practice empathy, you often get a warm response from others. This can strengthen friendships and make you feel more positive about your communication style. People may come to you for advice or simply trust you more because you show genuine care. This trust can circle back to boost your self-esteem since you see that your words have a good impact.

13. Communication Styles: Passive, Assertive, and Aggressive

13.1 Passive Style

Passive communicators often go along with what others want, rarely voicing their own needs or opinions. They might avoid conflict to the point of letting people walk over them. While staying quiet might keep the peace for a while, it can lead to frustration and low self-esteem because their concerns are never addressed.

13.2 Assertive Style

Assertive communicators state their thoughts clearly and respectfully. They listen to others but also expect to be heard. For example, an assertive teen might say, "I understand your point, but I need you to know how I feel as well." This style is generally the healthiest for building confidence and maintaining respectful relationships.

13.3 Aggressive Style

Aggressive communicators use threats, yelling, or insults to get their way. This style often leads to fear or resentment in others. While an aggressive person might feel powerful for a moment, it usually damages relationships and does not foster real respect.

13.4 Practicing Assertiveness

If you find yourself leaning toward passive or aggressive styles, it can help to practice assertive phrases. For instance, if a friend wants to borrow your belongings, but you are not comfortable, you might say, "I understand you need to use it, but I'm not okay with lending it out right now." This approach states your boundary clearly without attacking the other person.

---

14. Practicing Communication Every Day

14.1 Small Steps

Improving communication is not just about big speeches or major conflicts. It also involves daily interactions like greeting classmates with eye contact or telling your parents how your day went. These small habits build up over time and help you feel more at ease with speaking and listening.

14.2 Self-Recording

One practical method is to record yourself talking, perhaps while practicing a presentation or even just explaining your day. Then, watch or listen to yourself. Notice any signs of nervousness, such as saying "um" a lot or avoiding looking up. Take note of what you do well, too—maybe you have a good pace or a friendly tone. By doing this regularly, you can monitor your growth.

14.3 Role-Play with Friends

You could also practice communication scenarios with a trusted friend. For example, pretend one of you is a teacher, and the other needs help with an assignment. Or act out a situation where you must refuse a favor. Role-playing allows you to try different approaches safely. Your friend can give you feedback on how you came across, and you can do the same for them.

Chapter 6: Building Positive Friendships

1. Introduction

Friendships are a significant part of teenage life. Your friends can influence how you spend your time, what values you hold, and even how you feel about yourself. Friendships can give you a sense of belonging and support. They can also cause heartbreak if you get into conflicts, face betrayal, or grow apart. For teen girls striving for confidence, choosing and nurturing friendships can be especially important.

This chapter will guide you through understanding what makes a healthy friendship. We will explore traits of good friends, ways to spot negative patterns, and strategies for strengthening bonds with people who make you feel good about yourself. We will also talk about setting boundaries, handling peer pressure, and addressing conflicts that may arise. By the end, you should have a clearer picture of how to form friendships that add joy and growth to your life rather than stress and doubt.

2. Why Friendships Matter for Confidence

2.1 Emotional Support

A good friend is someone you can lean on when you are upset or stressed. They can offer a kind ear, helpful words, or simply the comfort of knowing you are not alone. This emotional support can lessen self-doubt and remind you that someone values you, which in turn boosts your self-confidence.

2.2 Shared Experiences

Friends often share many experiences, like attending the same school events or enjoying similar hobbies. These shared moments can deepen your connection and create memories that make you feel more at ease with who you are. Feeling accepted by someone who truly understands you can help you accept yourself more as well.

2.3 Growth Opportunities

Quality friends challenge you in a positive way. They might push you to try new activities or encourage you to go for your goals. Having someone believe in you makes it easier to take risks, like joining a new club or speaking up in class. Over time, these small steps build a foundation of self-trust.

2.4 Lowered Stress

Knowing there is at least one person who "gets" you can make tough days feel more manageable. Even simple acts, like texting a friend to vent about a test, can reduce tension. This lower stress level helps keep your mind clearer, which benefits your confidence.

---

3. Qualities of a Good Friend

3.1 Trustworthy

Trust is the backbone of any solid friendship. You should feel safe sharing your thoughts or problems without worrying that your friend will spread them around. A trustworthy friend keeps your secrets, tells you the truth when needed, and respects your boundaries.

3.2 Supportive

Support can mean different things. Sometimes a supportive friend just listens without judging. Other times, they might offer advice, help you prepare for a big event, or cheer you on at a game. Importantly, a supportive friend does not pressure you to do things you dislike or that could harm you.

3.3 Respectful

Respect means treating each other as individuals with your own opinions and limits. A respectful friend does not put you down, call you names, or mock your interests. They also understand when you need space or time to yourself.

3.4 Honest and Kind

Honesty is about being truthful, but it should be paired with kindness. Sometimes a friend might need to point out something you need to work on, but they can do so gently. For example, if you are acting distant, a caring friend might ask if something is bothering you rather than accusing you of being rude.

---

4. Different Types of Friendships

4.1 Acquaintances

These are people you know but are not very close to. You might say "hi" in the hallway or chat about surface-level topics. Acquaintances can become closer friends over time, or they may remain casual contacts.

4.2 Casual Friends

Casual friends are those you hang out with occasionally, like in a club or at lunch. You might discuss certain interests or subjects, but you do not share deeper personal matters. These friendships can still be enjoyable and light-hearted.

4.3 Close Friends

Close friends are the people you trust most. You can confide in them about personal issues, and they feel comfortable doing the same. You usually spend more time together, know each other's families, and keep in touch regularly. These are the friendships that have a strong impact on your confidence and emotional life.

4.4 Online Friends

With the rise of social media, many teens form online-only friendships. While these can be meaningful, it is wise to be cautious. Make sure any online friend is who they claim to be, and do not share too much private information until you are certain of their trustworthiness.

---

5. Identifying Negative Friendship Patterns

5.1 Signs of a Harmful Friendship

- **Constant Criticism:** If your friend regularly puts you down or makes jokes at your expense, that is not healthy.
- **Ignoring Boundaries:** If you ask them not to share something personal, but they do anyway, they are ignoring your boundaries.
- **Dishonesty:** Repeated lies or half-truths erode trust.
- **Manipulation:** A friend who pressures you to do things you do not feel comfortable with is crossing a line.

5.2 Emotional Ups and Downs

Some friendships have a lot of drama, which can leave you emotionally exhausted. One day, they treat you well, and the next, they give you the cold shoulder without explanation. This inconsistency can lower your self-esteem and cause anxiety. Healthy friendships can have disagreements but do not constantly leave you feeling unsure about where you stand.

5.3 Recognizing Toxic Behavior

A toxic friend may use guilt, blame, or fear to control you. They might threaten to leave you out if you do not do what they want. They might embarrass you in front of others or compare you negatively to themselves. If you find that a friendship is making you doubt your worth more than it helps you feel good, it might be toxic.

---

6. Making New Friends

6.1 Overcoming Shyness

If you are shy, it can feel daunting to talk to new people. Try starting with small steps, like smiling at someone in class or asking a simple question about homework. These little actions can spark a conversation. Over time, you might find that you share an interest or a sense of humor, opening the door to a potential friendship.

6.2 Joining Clubs or Activities

One of the best ways to meet new friends is to join clubs or extracurricular activities that interest you. If you love art, sports, or science, you are more likely to find like-minded people by being around those topics. The shared activity gives you something to talk about, reducing awkwardness.

6.3 Online Communities

While caution is necessary, there are safe online communities or forums for specific hobbies or causes. Engaging in these can help you meet people from different backgrounds who share your passions. Just remember not to share personal details like your full address or phone number until you fully trust them.

6.4 Approaching Potential Friends

If there is someone you find interesting, do not be afraid to start a conversation. You might say something like, "Hey, I noticed your notebook has a cool design. Where did you get it?" or "You seem really good at that. Do you have any tips?" People often appreciate genuine curiosity. Even if they are not interested in a deeper connection, most will respond kindly to friendly questions.

---

7. Strengthening Existing Friendships

7.1 Quality Time

Friendships thrive when you spend meaningful time together. This could be studying side by side, playing a game, or simply sharing a relaxed moment watching movies. Make an effort to schedule time with friends, even if it is short. Consistency helps maintain strong bonds.

7.2 Shared Goals

Working on a shared goal can bring friends closer. Maybe you both want to improve at a sport, learn an instrument, or volunteer. Pushing each other, sharing progress, and celebrating small wins along the way can deepen your connection.

7.3 Genuine Compliments

Let your friend know what you appreciate about them. Maybe they are patient, or they have a great sense of humor. Sincere compliments can brighten someone's day and show that you value them. This, in turn, often inspires them to show care for you too.

7.4 Supporting Each Other Through Challenges

When friends face hardships—like a tough exam, a breakup, or family issues—your support can make a big difference. Offer to listen or just be there. Ask what they need. Show them that you believe in their ability to handle the challenge. This shows loyalty and kindness, which often strengthens trust in the friendship.

8. Setting Boundaries with Friends

8.1 Understanding Personal Limits

Boundaries are the lines you draw around your comfort zone. These can be physical (like needing personal space) or emotional (like not wanting to talk about certain topics). Healthy friendships respect these lines. For example, if you say you need alone time, a respectful friend will understand instead of making you feel guilty.

8.2 How to Communicate Boundaries

1. **Use Clear Statements:** Instead of hinting, say exactly what you need. For instance, "I need some quiet time right now" or "I'm not comfortable sharing that detail."
2. **Stay Firm, Not Rude:** You can protect your boundaries while being kind in your tone.
3. **Suggest Alternatives:** If a friend wants something you cannot offer, you might suggest another option that works for both of you.

8.3 Respecting Others' Boundaries

Friendships go both ways. Just as you have your limits, your friends have theirs. Learning to respect their comfort zones is a sign of true friendship and maturity. This might mean understanding when they want to do something without you, or not pushing them to talk about a subject that makes them upset.

9. Peer Pressure and How to Handle It

9.1 Recognizing Peer Pressure

Peer pressure occurs when your friend group tries to make you do something you do not want to do. This can be direct, like someone saying, "You have to join us, or you are not cool," or indirect, such as everyone else doing it and you feel left out. Peer pressure can involve activities like skipping class, trying substances, or teasing someone else.

9.2 Evaluating the Risks

Before giving in to peer pressure, think about the potential consequences. Could it harm your health, your record at school, or your sense of right and wrong? Sometimes, just pausing to consider outcomes is enough to realize you do not want to go through with it.

9.3 Standing Up to Pressure

You can firmly say no while being polite. For instance, "I understand that's what you want to do, but I'm not comfortable with it." If they keep pushing, you have the right to walk away or call someone you trust. True friends should respect your choices, even if they do not agree with them.

9.4 Choosing Friends Who Respect You

Sometimes, the best way to avoid harmful peer pressure is to spend time with people who share your values or at least respect them. If a friend group regularly does things that make you uneasy, it might be time to step back. You deserve friends who support your well-being, not those who put it at risk.

10. Dealing with Friendship Conflicts

10.1 Causes of Conflict

Even close friends can argue. Common triggers include jealousy, misunderstandings, competition, or feeling that one person is ignoring the other. Conflicts do not mean the friendship has to end. Often, they can be opportunities to learn more about each other's feelings and boundaries.

10.2 Conflict Resolution Steps

1. **Calm Down First:** If you are angry or hurt, take time to cool off.
2. **Talk in Private:** Avoid sorting out personal issues in front of a large group or on social media.
3. **Use "I" Statements:** Rather than accusing your friend, explain how you feel. For example, "I felt left out when you went to the event without telling me."
4. **Listen to Their Side:** Hear what your friend says about the situation. Sometimes, they did not realize how they affected you.
5. **Find a Solution:** Work together to figure out how to avoid the same conflict in the future.

10.3 Knowing When to Let Go

If conflicts keep happening and the friendship causes more pain than joy, it might be time to move on. While letting go can be sad, it can also free you to find healthier connections. Your emotional health matters, and sometimes stepping away is the best choice for both of you.

---

11. Long-Distance Friendships

11.1 Staying in Touch

When a close friend moves away, or you do, it can be tough. But technology makes it easier to stay connected. You can schedule video calls, write emails, or even send letters if you like something more personal. Consistency in communication can keep the friendship alive, even if you cannot see each other in person.

11.2 Accepting Changes

People grow and change, especially during the teen years. Long-distance friends might develop new interests or meet new people you have never heard of. Instead of feeling left out, show curiosity about their new life. Share updates about your own life. Accept that the friendship may feel different but can still be meaningful.

11.3 Visiting and Future Plans

If possible, plan visits during holidays or special weekends. Even if these visits are short, they can bring you closer. Also, think about future plans. Maybe you can go to a music festival together or apply to the same college. Having something to look forward to can keep the bond strong despite the distance.

---

12. Balancing Friendships and Other Responsibilities

12.1 Time Management

Friendships take time, but so do homework, family duties, and personal relaxation. Finding a balance is key. You can create a simple schedule to divide your day or week. For instance, set aside certain hours for studying and certain hours for socializing. This helps you keep your grades up while still having fun with friends.

12.2 Avoiding Burnout

Sometimes people feel pressured to hang out with friends all the time to avoid missing out. But too much socializing can be draining. It is okay to say no to a plan if you need to rest or catch up on tasks. Real friends will understand if you explain you need some downtime.

12.3 Communicating Your Limits

If you are feeling overwhelmed, talk to your friends. Let them know you value their company but have other duties too. You might say, "I really want to go out this Friday, but I also have a big test. Can we meet earlier so I have time to study later?" Good friends will respect that you have responsibilities and encourage you to do well.

---

13. The Role of Friends in Building Your Identity

13.1 Finding Like-Minded Individuals

Sometimes you discover new interests because of a friend who introduces you to something. Friends can shape your tastes in music, fashion, or hobbies. Be open to learning from them, but also feel free to decide if something is not your style. It is your life, and you do not have to adopt every preference they have.

13.2 Getting Different Perspectives

Your friends might come from various backgrounds and have different views on life. Hearing their perspectives can broaden your mind. You may see new ways of thinking about problems or realize there is more than one path to a solution. This openness can enrich your self-confidence because you see there is room for your unique views as well.

13.3 Avoiding Negative Influence

While friends can shape you positively, they can also sway you in harmful ways. If a friend group criticizes your goals or makes fun of your personal growth, that might hold you back. A healthy friendship should allow you to explore your interests and support your decisions, even if they do not share the same path.

---

14. Helping a Friend in Need

14.1 Recognizing Signs of Struggle

Sometimes your friend might be going through a hard time—depression, anxiety, family troubles, or even just a strong feeling of sadness. Look out for changes in behavior, like they stop texting as much, skip outings, or seem unusually quiet. Approach them gently and ask if something is on their mind.

14.2 Offering Support Without Judgment

Let your friend know you are there to listen. Avoid immediately giving them solutions or telling them what they "should" do, as that might feel pushy. Instead, ask, "Would you like to talk about it?" or "Is there anything I can do to help?" If they are not ready to share, simply saying you care can be comforting.

14.3 Encouraging Professional Help

If you suspect your friend is dealing with serious issues, such as self-harm or severe mental health problems, encourage them to talk to a counselor, therapist, or trusted adult. Offer to go with them for support if that helps. While you can be a good friend, some problems need professional intervention.

Chapter 7: Handling Stress

1. Introduction

Stress is a normal part of life, but as a teen girl, you may find it especially hard to manage. There are many sources of stress, like school, relationships, or even future plans. Sometimes, stress can feel overwhelming, making you wonder if you can keep up. The good news is that there are simple, practical steps you can take to deal with stress in a healthy way. By learning these methods, you can protect your mental health and maintain your confidence.

In this chapter, we will discuss where stress comes from, ways it can affect you, and techniques to help you feel calmer. We will look at daily habits that lower stress, methods for handling sudden bursts of worry, and ideas for long-term balance. You will also learn how to identify when stress is becoming too much and what to do in those moments. The goal is not to get rid of all stress—some stress can actually help motivate you—but to manage it so it does not control your life.

2. Understanding Stress

2.1 What Is Stress?

Stress is your body's response to challenges or demands. It can come from everyday events, like having too much homework, or from bigger changes, such as moving to a new school. When you face a situation that feels challenging, your body and mind become more alert. This is often called the "fight or flight" response, which originally helped humans react to danger. However, in modern life, stress might come from social pressure or fear of failing a test, and your body might still react as though it is in serious danger.

A little stress can be helpful. For example, you may feel a burst of energy that makes you study harder or do well in a sports match. But too much stress over a long period can harm your emotional and physical well-being.

2.2 Types of Stress

1. **Acute Stress:** This is short-term stress that appears suddenly and goes away quickly. For instance, feeling nervous about speaking in front of the class. After you finish, the stress often subsides.
2. **Chronic Stress:** This is long-term stress that stays for weeks or months. It might come from ongoing problems at home or repeated difficulties at school. Chronic stress can harm your health if not handled properly.
3. **Episodic Stress:** This happens when you have repeated episodes of acute stress. Maybe you often face deadlines at school or constant social drama. Even though each incident is short, having many stress spikes can wear you down.

2.3 Common Stressors for Teen Girls

- **School Pressure:** Exams, homework, and the push to get good grades.
- **Social Issues:** Conflicts with friends, fear of being left out, or peer pressure to act in certain ways.
- **Family Struggles:** Arguments with parents or siblings, financial worries at home, or lack of support.
- **Self-Doubt:** Fear of not meeting personal goals or comparing yourself to others.
- **Busy Schedules:** Trying to balance school, part-time jobs, sports, or clubs can cause a constant feeling of rush.

Recognizing what causes you stress is the first step. Once you know your triggers, you can plan how to handle them, rather than letting them overwhelm you.

---

3. How Stress Affects Your Mind and Body

3.1 Emotional Effects

- **Irritability:** Feeling easily annoyed by small things.
- **Anxiety:** Worrying too much about future events or imagining worst-case scenarios.
- **Sadness or Hopelessness:** A lingering sense that things will not get better.
- **Low Motivation:** Finding it hard to start tasks because the stress makes everything feel heavier.

3.2 Physical Effects

- **Headaches or Stomachaches:** Ongoing stress can cause tension headaches or digestive problems.
- **Fatigue:** Feeling unusually tired, even if you sleep enough.
- **Sleep Problems:** Trouble falling asleep or staying asleep because your mind is busy worrying.
- **Muscle Tension:** Stress can make your shoulders, neck, or back feel tight or sore.

3.3 Impact on Daily Life

When stress piles up, it can affect your performance at school, your relationships with friends and family, and your overall self-confidence. You might feel too anxious to speak up in class or too tired to hang out with friends. Over time, these problems can lower your mood and make you doubt yourself.

4. Healthy Lifestyle Habits to Reduce Stress

4.1 Regular Sleep

Sleep gives your mind and body time to recharge. Experts often suggest teens aim for 8 to 10 hours of sleep. When you do not get enough rest, stress can build more easily. Try to keep a consistent bedtime, and avoid screens (like your phone or tablet) at least 30 minutes before sleeping. The blue light from screens can trick your brain into staying alert.

4.2 Balanced Eating

Your body needs a variety of nutrients to function well, including those that affect mood. While it is okay to have snacks, try to include fruits, vegetables, whole grains, and protein in your daily meals. Avoid too much caffeine or sugar, as they can make you jittery or result in energy crashes later.

4.3 Regular Physical Activity

You do not have to be a top athlete to benefit from movement. Activities like walking, stretching, or dancing can release tension. Exercise also causes your body to produce endorphins, which can improve your mood. Even 20 minutes of moderate activity a few days a week can make a difference in how you handle stress.

4.4 Time in Nature

Spending time outdoors can calm your mind. A simple walk in a park or sitting under a tree can help you reset. If you live in a city, look for green spaces or places where you can see the sky, get fresh air, and momentarily step away from your routine.

5. Mind-Based Techniques for Handling Stress

5.1 Deep Breathing Exercises

When you feel a rush of anxiety, try this simple method:

1. Inhale through your nose for a count of four.
2. Hold your breath for a count of four.
3. Exhale through your mouth for a count of four.
4. Repeat several times.

Deep breathing tells your brain to relax, slowing your heart rate and helping you feel calmer. It is quick and can be done anywhere—at home, in school, or even on the bus.

5.2 Simple Relaxation Practice

- **Find a Quiet Spot:** Sit or lie down in a comfortable position.
- **Close Your Eyes:** Take a few slow breaths.
- **Tense and Release Muscles:** Starting with your toes, tense them for a few seconds, then let go. Move up to your calves, thighs, and so on, ending with your shoulders and jaw.
- **Stay Still for a Moment:** Notice how your body feels lighter after releasing tension.

This practice helps your muscles remember what relaxation feels like. You can do it before bed or anytime you are feeling stressed.

5.3 Writing in a Journal

Putting your thoughts on paper can help clear your mind. Write about what is bothering you, or list things that went well that day. Some people also like to write down what they are grateful for, as this can shift the focus away from stress toward positive aspects of life. Journaling does not need to be fancy—just be honest with yourself.

5.4 Guided Imagery

Close your eyes and picture a place that makes you feel at ease—a beach, a cozy room, or a spot in nature. Imagine the details, like the sounds, smells, and colors. Spend a few minutes immersing yourself in this mental scene. This method can calm racing thoughts and slow your heartbeat.

---

6. Time Management to Lower Stress

6.1 Planning Your Day

A lot of stress comes from feeling that you do not have enough time. Creating a simple plan for your day can give you a sense of control. Write down your tasks and activities, estimate how much time each will take, and decide what is most important. Having a clear list can reduce the worry that you might forget something or run out of time.

6.2 Setting Priorities

If your schedule is packed, learn to separate what must be done from what can wait. For example, finishing a project due tomorrow is more urgent than organizing your room. By ranking your tasks, you can address the high-priority items first, which helps lower anxiety about unfinished work.

6.3 Breaking Tasks Down

Large tasks can feel overwhelming. Split them into smaller steps. For example, if you have a term paper, break it into stages: research, outline, first draft, editing. Tackle each step one by one, and you will feel a small sense of achievement after each stage. This method makes huge tasks seem more manageable.

6.4 Avoiding Procrastination

Procrastination is putting off tasks until the last minute. It might feel good in the short term, but it usually increases stress in the long run. Try studying or working on big assignments a little each day. Even 15-20 minutes of focused effort can add up, and you will feel less pressure as the deadline approaches.

---

7. Social Support

7.1 Talking to Friends

Friends can offer a listening ear and help you feel less alone. When you share your worries, you might discover they have faced similar problems. However, it is important to choose someone you trust. If you sense a friend is not supportive or tends to spread private information, be cautious about sharing too much.

7.2 Family Support

If you have a good relationship with your parents, guardians, or siblings, lean on them. They might give advice based on their own life experience. If home is a source of stress, find small ways to communicate your feelings calmly. For example, explain what you are going through and ask if there is a way they can help reduce some of the pressure.

7.3 Teachers and Counselors

Teachers and counselors at school are there to help you learn and grow. If school stress is high, let them know. Teachers may give you tips on how to study smarter, and counselors can offer strategies to handle academic or personal issues. They can also connect you with resources outside of school if needed.

7.4 Support Groups or Clubs

Some schools have clubs that focus on mental health or specific hobbies. Joining such groups can connect you with others who share your interests or challenges. Feeling like you belong to a supportive community can reduce stress and remind you that you are not alone.

8. Handling Sudden Stress or Panic

8.1 Recognizing the Signs

Sudden stress often comes with a racing heartbeat, quick breathing, and a feeling of being trapped. Your mind may fill with frightening thoughts or you may feel shaky. Recognizing these signs early can help you apply quick calming techniques.

8.2 Quick Calm-Down Steps

1. **Stop and Breathe:** Pause what you are doing, close your eyes if possible, and take a few slow, deep breaths.
2. **Grounding:** Focus on your senses. Name five things you can see, four you can touch, three you can hear, two you can smell, and one you can taste (or would like to taste). This method brings your attention to the present moment.
3. **Positive Self-Talk:** Repeat a simple phrase like, "I'm okay, this will pass," or, "I can handle this." This can disrupt negative thoughts.

8.3 Physical Release

If you can, move around. Shake out your arms or take a quick walk to release some of the tension. Physical action can help break the cycle of panic and bring your breathing back to normal.

---

9. Long-Term Stress Management

9.1 Recognizing Patterns

Pay attention to when you feel stressed most often. Is it always on Sunday evenings before school starts again? Is it when you are running late? Once you see patterns, you can take action to minimize them. For instance, you might set your clothes and backpack ready the night before to reduce morning stress.

9.2 Building Resilience

Resilience means being able to recover from setbacks. One way to build it is by seeing challenges as temporary rather than permanent. For example, if you fail a test, it does not mean you are a failure overall. You can study harder or seek help next time. Each time you get through a tough situation, your resilience grows, making future stresses easier to handle.

9.3 Limiting Negative Influences

Sometimes you might face stress from social media, toxic friendships, or too many commitments. Learn to set boundaries where possible. You could limit social media use if it makes you anxious about your appearance or life compared to others. You might step back from friendships that drag you into drama. Simplifying your life can greatly lower ongoing stress.

9.4 Keeping a Positive Outlook

While you cannot change every stressful situation, you can change how you respond. Try to look for solutions rather than dwelling on worst-case outcomes. This does not mean ignoring problems, but rather focusing on how you can address them. A balanced view—seeing both the difficulties and what you can do about them—often reduces tension.

---

10. When Stress Becomes Too Much

10.1 Signs You Need More Help

- **Constant Worry or Sadness:** You feel anxious or down most of the time.
- **Drop in Daily Functioning:** You cannot concentrate at all, or you avoid activities you once enjoyed.

- **Physical Symptoms:** Stomachaches, headaches, or fatigue become a daily problem.
- **Harmful Thoughts:** If you ever think about hurting yourself or feel hopeless about the future, this is a serious sign you need professional help immediately.

10.2 Where to Seek Help

- **School Counselor:** They can listen, offer coping methods, and connect you to other services if necessary.
- **Doctor or Therapist:** Professional mental health experts can guide you through stress and anxiety. They might use talk-based methods or suggest other resources.
- **Hotlines:** In many places, there are phone or text lines you can reach out to if you are in distress. These lines are usually staffed by trained volunteers or counselors.

10.3 Reaching Out Is Brave

It might feel scary to tell someone you are struggling, but it shows courage and self-respect. Everybody needs help sometimes, and asking for it does not make you weak—it shows you want to take care of yourself. By reaching out, you can get the support you need to manage stress in a healthier way.

---

11. Practical Exercises to Put It All Together

11.1 Daily Stress Check

Each evening, ask yourself:

1. **What was stressful today?**
2. **What worked to handle it?**
3. **What will I try next time?**

This quick review helps you see progress and adjust your methods. Over time, you will notice patterns and learn which strategies suit you best.

11.2 Week-Long Challenge

Pick one stress-reducing technique, like deep breathing or journaling, and practice it daily for a week. Note any changes in your mood or sleep. If you see improvement, keep it going. If not, try another method. This trial-and-error approach helps you build your own stress-management toolbox.

11.3 Rewarding Healthy Stress Relief

When you use a healthy way to calm down—like taking a break, going for a walk, or doing breathing exercises—recognize that you made a good choice. Remind yourself that you chose to protect your well-being. Over time, your brain starts to link these positive actions with feeling better, making you more likely to use them in the future.

Chapter 8: Body Image

1. Introduction

Body image is how you view your body and how you think others see it. During your teen years, your body may go through many changes, and it is common to feel unsure about how you look. You might compare yourself to peers or see images in media that make you question if you measure up. These doubts can affect how you feel about yourself, leading to low confidence and sometimes harmful habits.

This chapter explores the idea of body image, where negative thoughts can come from, and ways to develop a healthier view of yourself. We will talk about the influence of social media and friends, as well as practical steps to care for your body without harsh self-criticism. By the end, you will have tools to look at your body in a kinder way, accept what makes you unique, and focus on your overall well-being instead of chasing unrealistic ideals.

2. What Shapes Body Image?

2.1 Media and Social Influences

Movies, TV shows, and social media often present a narrow idea of what is "perfect." Photos can be edited or show only the best angles. It is easy to forget that these images are not the full reality. Comparing yourself to a filtered photo online can make you feel less confident, even though the image may not be genuine.

2.2 Family and Friends

Comments from family members, even if they are meant to help, can affect how you see yourself. Phrases like "You should eat less" or "You are too thin" can linger in your mind. Friends might also influence your body image, whether they are joking about appearances or praising certain body types.

Being around people who talk constantly about dieting or looks can heighten your insecurities.

2.3 Personal Expectations

Sometimes the strongest pressure comes from within. You might think, "I have to be a certain weight," or "I must have perfect skin." These personal rules can be tough to meet and can create ongoing stress. Recognizing these internal pressures is the first step toward adjusting them to be more realistic and kind.

---

3. Effects of Negative Body Image

3.1 Emotional Harm

If you constantly feel your body is not good enough, you may experience sadness, anxiety, or a drop in self-esteem. These feelings can make you avoid social situations, such as parties or pool days, because you worry about how others will see you.

3.2 Unhealthy Behaviors

Negative body image can push people toward harmful behaviors:

- **Extreme Dieting:** Trying to drastically limit calories or skipping meals can harm your health.
- **Over-Exercising:** Working out too much in order to reach a specific body shape can lead to injury or burnout.
- **Hiding Your Body:** Wearing overly baggy clothes or refusing to participate in activities like swimming, just to avoid showing your body.

3.3 Strained Relationships

When body worries take over, it might be hard to fully connect with friends or enjoy everyday fun. You could end up talking about your insecurities all the time or avoiding events where you think your appearance might be judged. This focus on self-criticism can push people away or limit your social life.

4. Challenging Unrealistic Beauty Standards

4.1 Recognizing Image Editing

Social media pictures are often edited or staged. Influencers and celebrities may have entire teams helping them look a certain way. Lighting, makeup, and camera angles can totally change how someone appears. Many images you see online are not a fair basis for comparison, since they do not show life in its real form.

4.2 Spotting Media Tricks

Some magazines or ads create a "perfect" body by editing out any natural features like wrinkles, stretch marks, or body hair. Once you realize how common these tricks are, you can better understand that these images do not represent real life. This awareness can help you be kinder to yourself when you look in the mirror.

4.3 Different Body Types

Humans come in many shapes and sizes, and there is no single shape that is best. Your body type might be influenced by genetics or other factors beyond your control. Rather than trying to fit into a mold, aim to keep your body healthy in ways that work best for you. This can involve balanced eating, moving regularly, and caring for your mental well-being.

5. Building a Healthier Body Image

5.1 Practicing Body Gratitude

Instead of focusing on what your body lacks, try listing things you appreciate about it. Maybe you like that your legs are strong enough to take long walks, or that your hands let you draw or play an instrument. Recognizing these good things can shift your attention from looks to function, helping you see that your body does many useful tasks.

5.2 Choosing Comfortable Clothing

Wear clothes that fit well and feel good. Sometimes, people try to squeeze into styles that do not suit their shape or comfort level, leading to frustration. When you are comfortable, you can focus more on enjoying your day rather than worrying about how your outfit looks.

5.3 Positive Self-Talk About Your Body

If you catch yourself thinking, "I hate my shape," pause and rephrase it as something more realistic, like, "I am not happy with this part of my body, but I can treat it with kindness." You can also say, "I am more than just my looks—I have many qualities to offer." Over time, these small changes in language can influence how you feel about yourself.

5.4 Avoiding "Fat Talk"

Sometimes, friends or family bond by insulting their own bodies, saying things like, "I look so bad today," in front of the mirror. This is often called "fat talk," but it applies to any negative comment about your body. Try not to join these conversations. If your friends do this, you might gently change the subject or point out something positive instead.

---

6. Healthy Approaches to Eating and Activity

6.1 Balanced Eating, Not Restrictive Dieting

Aim to eat a variety of foods: fruits, vegetables, grains, and proteins. It is fine to enjoy treats, too. Focus on balance rather than strict rules. Restrictive diets can lead to nutrient deficiencies, low energy, and a troubled view of food. If you need help with nutrition, consider talking to a registered dietitian or a doctor rather than following trends found online.

6.2 Enjoyable Exercise

Pick physical activities you actually like. Maybe you prefer dancing in your room, riding a bike with friends, or playing a team sport. Regular movement is important for health, but it should not become a punishment for eating or a way to achieve a certain body shape. When you choose activities you enjoy, exercise feels like a natural part of life rather than a chore.

6.3 Staying Hydrated

Drinking water supports overall health, keeps your skin in good condition, and helps you feel more energetic. If plain water is boring to you, try adding slices of fruit or opting for caffeine-free teas. Avoid going overboard on sugary drinks, as they can affect energy levels and mood.

---

7. Media Literacy: Handling Social Media Pressure

7.1 Curating Your Feed

You have some control over what you see on social media. If certain accounts constantly make you feel bad about yourself, you can unfollow or mute them. Instead, follow pages that promote positivity, healthy habits, or creative interests. Surrounding yourself with encouraging content can reduce daily body-image stress.

7.2 Taking Breaks

It is easy to get pulled into scrolling for hours, looking at photos of people who seem perfect. This can damage your self-esteem. Schedule "social media breaks" where you go offline for a certain period each day. Use that time to read, draw, play outside, or talk to friends in person. Stepping away can give you a clearer view of what really matters in your life.

7.3 Fact-Checking and Realism

When you see a before-and-after post or a picture of someone who claims they got results overnight, ask yourself how realistic it is. Some people use filters, angles, or editing to exaggerate changes. Being aware that not everything you see is true can protect you from feeling inadequate.

---

8. Handling Body-Related Comments

8.1 Responding to Unwanted Opinions

Sometimes people make remarks about your appearance, whether it is a compliment that feels uncomfortable or a rude comment. You can respond calmly, like, "I appreciate your concern, but I'm comfortable with how I look." If the comment is mean, you have the right to ignore it or walk away. You do not owe anyone a detailed explanation about your body.

8.2 Dealing with Teasing or Bullying

If someone bullies you about your looks, it can be painful. Try these steps:

1. **Stay Composed:** Do not show them the reaction they might be trying to provoke.
2. **Speak Up or Seek Help:** Tell a teacher, counselor, or trusted adult. Bullying is not okay, and you deserve support.
3. **Talk to Friends:** Lean on those who respect you. Often, friends can stand by you, making you feel less isolated.

8.3 Setting Personal Boundaries

You can kindly ask people not to comment on your body. For instance, "I'd rather not discuss my weight, thanks." This is especially important with family or friends who may think they are helping but are actually causing stress. Stating your boundary can remind them that your body is your personal matter.

---

9. Building Inner Confidence Beyond Looks

9.1 Exploring Your Interests

Spend time on hobbies or activities that have nothing to do with appearance. It could be music, coding, art, or volunteering. The more you develop skills and passions, the more you see your worth in other areas. This broader view of yourself can lessen the weight you put on looks alone.

9.2 Celebrating Personal Growth

When you learn a new skill or overcome a challenge, take a moment to recognize that progress. Maybe you learned how to cook a new dish or improved your math grade. These achievements show that you are growing, and they can help shift your focus from how your body looks to what you can do with it.

9.3 Giving Back

Helping others can boost how you feel about yourself. You might volunteer at a community event, tutor a younger student, or join a charity fundraiser. Realizing you can make a difference in someone else's life highlights the fact that your value goes far beyond your physical appearance.

---

10. Support Systems for Body Positivity

10.1 Talking to Trusted Adults

If you struggle with how you see your body, talk to a parent, teacher, or counselor you trust. They might share their own experiences or offer advice on how to cope with outside pressures. Sometimes, just saying your worries out loud can help you see them in a more balanced way.

10.2 Positive Friends and Groups

Surround yourself with friends who build you up rather than criticize or mock you. Seek out school clubs or community groups that value kindness and acceptance. If you find an online group, make sure it encourages healthy habits and does not pressure you to change your body in harmful ways.

10.3 Professional Guidance

If you constantly feel upset about your looks or if it starts to affect your eating or daily life, it might be helpful to see a mental health professional. Therapists can help you unlearn harmful thoughts, set healthier goals, and identify where negative feelings come from. This is not a sign of weakness, but of self-care.

---

11. Common Myths About Body Image

11.1 "Only Thin People Struggle with Body Image"

Body issues can affect anyone, whether thin, average, or plus-size. People of all shapes might feel pressure or anxiety about their looks. Body image stress does not discriminate based on size.

11.2 "If I Change My Body, I'll Love Myself"

Altering your body—through extreme diets or other methods—does not guarantee happiness. Often, deeper self-esteem problems remain. Focusing on self-acceptance and health is more likely to lead to lasting peace and confidence.

11.3 "Men Don't Care About Looks"

Society often says boys or men do not worry about appearance, but that is not true. They also feel pressure, just in different ways. Understanding that body image can affect everyone helps you see it as a broad issue, not just yours.

12. Activities to Develop a Positive Body Image

12.1 Mirror Exercises

When you see yourself in the mirror, try picking out at least one thing you appreciate. It might be the color of your eyes or the shape of your hands. This is not about vanity; it is about training your brain to see good aspects instead of focusing on flaws.

12.2 Art or Collage

Gather images or quotes that promote a healthy view of the body—pictures of people enjoying life, wearing colorful outfits, or being active in fun ways. Make a collage or a small mood board to look at whenever negative thoughts creep in. Seeing encouraging words and pictures can shift your mindset.

12.3 Positive Digital Space

Create a folder on your phone or computer with pictures of memories or notes that remind you of your strengths. Whenever you feel down about how you look, scroll through them. This can help break the cycle of negative self-talk.

13. Handling Setbacks in Body Positivity

13.1 Expect Ups and Downs

Learning to accept your body is not a one-time fix; it is a gradual process. There will be days when you feel good and days when you feel less confident. That is normal. Remind yourself that a single bad day does not erase the progress you have made.

13.2 Reaching Out

If you find yourself slipping into old habits of criticizing your appearance, talk to a friend or journal about what is happening. Share your worries instead of letting them grow in silence. Sometimes, just hearing someone else say, "I get it," can ease the self-doubt.

13.3 Adjusting Your Strategy

If certain activities or accounts on social media trigger negative feelings, it might be time to cut them out or limit them more. If you have tried the same coping methods without success, try a new approach—maybe a different counselor, a new hobby, or a different form of exercise.

---

14. Balancing Health Goals and Self-Acceptance

14.1 Setting Realistic Goals

It is okay to want to be stronger, more flexible, or have better endurance. However, these goals should be about health and personal growth, not about punishing your body or chasing a narrow image. Set goals you can measure, like running a bit farther each week or learning a new yoga pose.

14.2 Health as a Lifestyle, Not a Phase

Healthy eating and regular activity work best when they become part of your daily life. Crash diets or extreme workout plans usually do not last and can harm your body. Instead, find steady habits that you can keep up in the long run, like adding a vegetable to each meal or doing a fun physical activity a few times a week.

14.3 Listening to Your Body

Your body sends signals when it is hungry, tired, or stressed. Pay attention to those cues. If you are exhausted, allow yourself to rest instead of forcing a workout. If you are hungry, eat until you feel satisfied, rather than ignoring your hunger. Trusting these cues can help you maintain a balance that supports both mental and physical health.

Chapter 9: Setting and Reaching Goals

1. Introduction

Goals can guide you through your teen years. Whether you want to do better in school, improve a skill, or save money for something special, having specific aims gives you a sense of direction. Goals also help you measure your progress, see your growth, and feel more motivated. As you develop self-confidence, goals can reinforce that growth because you see real evidence of your hard work.

However, setting goals is one thing; reaching them is another. Some teens make ambitious plans but give up too soon. Others do not plan at all and instead rely on day-to-day chances. This chapter will show you practical ways to set realistic goals, keep track of your progress, handle setbacks, and find the motivation to keep going. By the end, you should have a clear idea of how to turn big dreams into achievable steps.

2. Why Goals Matter

2.1 Clarity of Direction

Imagine you have a map without a destination. You can wander, but you might not end up anywhere meaningful. Goals give you a sense of direction. If you want to improve in math, for example, you might set a goal to raise your test scores by a certain percentage. This target guides your study schedule and helps you focus.

2.2 Motivation Boost

Working toward something specific can energize you, especially on days you feel unmotivated. When you know exactly why you need to practice an instrument or study for an extra 30 minutes, it is easier to push yourself to do it. Goals can remind you that your efforts serve a purpose.

2.3 Sense of Achievement

Reaching a goal—no matter how small—can fill you with a sense of pride. It proves you can plan, work steadily, and see results. Each time you meet a goal, you add another layer of confidence to your self-image. This feeling can encourage you to set new aims, creating a positive cycle of effort and accomplishment.

---

3. Types of Goals

3.1 Short-Term Goals

Short-term goals often range from a few days to a few weeks. They could be as simple as finishing a book or improving a certain study habit for one exam. Because they are brief, they can give you quick "wins" that boost your motivation. For instance, deciding to do your homework as soon as you get home from school for one week is a short-term goal.

3.2 Medium-Term Goals

These goals can last a few months. For example, if you want to join a school competition in three months, you might set a medium-term goal to practice or prepare regularly until the event. You will still see progress along the way, but it requires more sustained effort than a short-term goal.

3.3 Long-Term Goals

Long-term goals can span from several months to years. Perhaps you want to attend a certain college or save a specific amount of money to buy something important. Long-term goals often require breaking down into smaller steps because they can feel overwhelming if you look at them all at once. Tracking your progress over time is key to staying on track with these bigger aims.

---

4. How to Set Effective Goals

4.1 Make Them Specific

Saying "I want to do better in school" is too broad. Instead, say "I want to raise my math grade from a C to a B by the end of the semester." This specific aim lets you plan exactly what you need to do—like studying 30 extra minutes each day or asking your teacher for practice problems.

4.2 Make Them Measurable

Adding numbers or measurable details helps you see progress. For instance, "I want to learn to play five new songs on the guitar in two months" is more concrete than "I want to get better at guitar." When you hit each milestone—like learning the first song—you will know you are making progress.

4.3 Keep Them Realistic

It is great to aim high, but if your goal is beyond what is feasible, you risk feeling disappointed. For example, planning to learn a complex musical piece in two days without any prior practice is likely not realistic. Make sure your goals are tough enough to stretch you but not so extreme that they are almost impossible.

4.4 Ensure They Are Relevant to You

Sometimes we set goals because friends, parents, or teachers suggest them, but they do not match our own passions. While external advice can be helpful, your goal should mean something to you personally. This personal connection keeps you motivated. If you truly care about it, you will put in the effort.

4.5 Give Them a Time Limit

Deadlines create a sense of urgency. If you just say, "I'll do it whenever," you might keep putting it off. A target date—like improving your math grade by the end of the semester—pushes you to get to work sooner rather than later. Just be careful to set a time frame that is neither too short nor too long.

---

5. Breaking Down Larger Goals

5.1 The Power of Small Steps

Large goals can be intimidating. If you want to write a 20-page paper, you might feel stressed about how to begin. Breaking it down into smaller steps can remove the fear and help you feel in control. For example:

1. Brainstorm your main idea.
2. Find five credible sources.
3. Create a rough outline.
4. Write the first draft of the introduction.
5. Write the main sections.
6. Edit and finalize.

As you finish each step, you see that you are moving closer to the final result. This method applies to many areas—like sports, music, learning a new language, or even a personal project.

5.2 Milestones and Checkpoints

Set milestones within your larger plan. For instance, if your goal is to get in better shape for a sports event in three months, you might decide to evaluate your progress every two weeks. At each checkpoint, note what has improved and what still needs work. This helps you stay aware of your development and avoid feeling lost.

5.3 Rewarding Progress

Each time you complete a step, acknowledge it. You do not need to do something major; a small treat or a relaxing activity can be enough to mark that you advanced. This keeps your mood high and reminds you that steady effort matters.

---

6. Staying Motivated

6.1 Visual Reminders

Some people like to put up goal trackers or simple charts on a wall or in their planner. For example, you can draw a progress bar that you color in whenever you move closer to a goal. Seeing this visual progress can spark motivation when your energy dips.

6.2 Accountability Partners

Find someone who supports your goal and can keep you on track. This could be a friend, sibling, or even a teacher. Share your goal with them and agree to check in regularly. Sometimes knowing someone will ask, "How's your progress?" is enough to keep you focused.

6.3 Positive Self-Talk

When working toward a goal, you might face doubt or setbacks. In these moments, how you speak to yourself matters. For instance, if you miss a few study sessions, instead of saying, "I can never stick to my plan," try, "I had a rough few days, but I can pick up again tomorrow." Small changes in your words can keep your outlook steady and solutions-oriented.

6.4 Connecting to Your "Why"

It is normal to lose motivation sometimes. To regain it, think about why the goal matters to you. Maybe it is about feeling proud of your academic progress, or perhaps learning a skill that can open doors in the future. Reminding yourself of the deeper reason can keep you going when the work feels tough.

---

7. Overcoming Obstacles

7.1 Handling Fear of Failure

Fear can stop you from even starting on a goal. You might worry, "What if I try and still fail?" Realize that not trying at all is already choosing to fail. Taking small steps—like practicing in a low-pressure setting—can ease your worry. Also, remember that failure can be a lesson. If you do not reach the goal on the first try, you often learn what to do differently next time.

7.2 Dealing with Time Constraints

Between school, family obligations, and social life, finding time to work toward your goal can be tough. Try to schedule a specific time each day or week to focus on it. Even 20 minutes of dedicated effort can add up over time. Keep track of your schedule to avoid double-booking yourself.

7.3 Lack of Resources

You might worry you do not have enough money, tools, or support. If your goal is to learn a certain software, but you cannot afford it, look for free versions or ask if your school offers resources. If you want to improve in a sport but cannot join a private league, maybe your school has a free or low-cost club. Creativity and persistence can help you find ways around resource limitations.

7.4 Comparing Yourself to Others

It is easy to look at classmates or friends who are further ahead and feel discouraged. But everyone's journey is different. Focus on your own improvement rather than racing others. If someone inspires you, see if you can learn from them instead of letting their success make you feel small.

---

8. Dealing with Setbacks and Adjusting Goals

8.1 Recognize When Something Is Not Working

If you have been trying to reach a goal for a while but are stuck, ask yourself if the plan needs adjusting. Maybe your steps are too large or your timeline is too short. Adjusting does not mean quitting. Instead, it shows that you are flexible enough to find a path that works better.

8.2 Learning from Mistakes

When something goes wrong, it can feel tempting to give up. However, mistakes can be valuable teachers. If you fail to reach a small milestone, examine why. Did you skip too many practice sessions? Did you aim too high for the time you had? Once you identify the problem, you can correct it and move forward smarter.

8.3 Re-Focusing on the Goal

Sometimes life changes. You might discover a new interest or face unforeseen events at home. In such cases, your original goal might become less important or less feasible. Revisit it and see if it still aligns with your interests and priorities. If not, it is okay to set a new, more relevant goal. Changing goals does not mean you failed; it means you are adapting to your current reality.

9. Examples of Goal-Setting in Everyday Life

9.1 Academic Goals

- **Improving Grades:** You could decide to raise your grade in one subject by a letter grade over the next marking period. Steps might include tutoring sessions, daily review, or talking to your teacher for extra practice.
- **Reading More Books:** If you love reading but never have time, set a target like reading for 20 minutes every night before bed. Keep track of the books you finish each month.

9.2 Personal Development Goals

- **Learning a New Skill:** Maybe you want to learn a new language or master a skill like painting. You could set a goal to complete a beginner-level online course within two months.
- **Building Confidence in Public Speaking:** You might aim to volunteer for one class presentation or read a short piece in front of a group once a month until you feel more at ease.

9.3 Physical Goals

- **Running a Certain Distance:** Set a goal to run or jog a specific distance without stopping, maybe a 5K or a mile. Create a weekly plan that steadily increases your running time or distance.
- **Flexible Body:** If you want to become more flexible, plan to stretch for 10 minutes every morning or practice short routines from reliable videos. Track small improvements, like how far you can reach.

9.4 Financial Goals

- **Saving Money:** If you get a small allowance or earn money from a part-time job, you might set a goal to save a certain amount each month. Keep it in a safe place or open a savings account. Over time, you can use this money for something important, like a bicycle or a trip.

- **Budgeting Skills:** Plan how much you will spend on snacks, outings, or hobbies, and stick to that plan. This way, you will learn money management early, which can be a big help in adulthood.

10. Practical Tools for Goal Tracking

10.1 Journals and Planners

A simple notebook or planner can help you keep track of daily tasks linked to your goal. You might jot down each day's progress, note challenges, and plan the next steps. Reviewing these notes at the end of the week helps you spot patterns.

10.2 Digital Apps

There are many free or low-cost apps that let you set goals, track habits, or schedule tasks. They can send reminders and show graphs of your progress. Pick one with features you like—maybe it awards points or badges for meeting daily targets.

10.3 Visual Boards

A poster or corkboard in your room can hold pictures, charts, or sticky notes related to your goals. For instance, if your goal is to improve in a sport, you could pin up pictures of athletes you admire, a training schedule, and a daily checklist. Seeing it each morning can inspire you to keep going.

11. Balancing Goals with Other Parts of Life

11.1 Avoiding Burnout

If you get overly focused on one goal, you might neglect other areas, like friendships, family time, or personal relaxation. Try to maintain balance. It is okay to work hard, but also remember to rest and have fun. Burnout happens when you push yourself so much that you lose energy and enjoyment.

11.2 Flexibility in Scheduling

Life can be unpredictable. You might face extra homework or family responsibilities. If you cannot follow your goal plan perfectly on some days, do not give up. Adjust your schedule when needed. A little progress is better than none.

11.3 Knowing When to Say "No"

Sometimes you will need to decline extra commitments if they interfere with your main priorities. For example, if your friend invites you to do something during your dedicated study time, you might say, "I need to finish my study hour, but I can join after that." Learning to say "no" politely but firmly can protect the time you have set aside for your goals.

Chapter 10: Healthy Relationships

1. Introduction

Relationships are central to our lives. We have relationships with family members, teachers, classmates, neighbors, and possibly romantic interests. Each relationship has its own dynamics. Some are supportive, some are complicated, and others might even be harmful. Understanding what makes a relationship healthy can help you choose the connections that boost your confidence rather than drag it down.

In this chapter, we will look at the signs of a healthy relationship, the importance of respect and communication, and how to recognize red flags. We will also talk about romantic relationships in a general sense, as many teens start exploring that area during these years. By the end, you will have a clearer idea of how to cultivate positive connections and protect yourself from harmful ones.

2. Different Types of Relationships

2.1 Family Relationships

This can include parents, step-parents, siblings, grandparents, or other relatives who are part of your household. Sometimes, families are very close and supportive. Other times, conflicts or misunderstandings can make these relationships tough. Learning to communicate your feelings can often improve things at home, but remember that some issues require outside help, like a counselor or a trusted family friend.

2.2 Friendships

We covered friendships in a previous chapter, but they are still part of the broader topic of relationships. Healthy friendships should help you feel accepted. You can share your worries, laugh together, and support each other's interests. Friendships may also face arguments or jealousy, but if both people handle conflicts respectfully, the friendship can remain strong.

2.3 Teacher-Student or Mentor-Mentee

Teachers, coaches, or mentors can influence your confidence. A good mentor believes in you and challenges you to grow. You can learn a lot from someone who guides you in a respectful and encouraging way. However, remember that the relationship should stay professional. If a teacher crosses boundaries or makes you uncomfortable, you have the right to speak up or report it.

2.4 Romantic or Dating Relationships

During the teen years, some people become curious about dating or having a romantic partner. Romantic relationships can teach you about intimacy, trust, and emotions. However, they can also be stressful if not handled with mutual respect and healthy communication. Your main focus should be on learning about yourself, understanding what you value, and ensuring you feel respected and safe.

---

3. Key Elements of a Healthy Relationship

3.1 Respect

Respect means you see the other person as an individual with their own thoughts, feelings, and rights. In a healthy relationship, respect goes both ways. You do not ignore someone's comfort level, and they do not ignore yours. For example, if you ask for some personal space, a respectful friend or partner will listen and avoid pressuring you.

3.2 Trust

Trust is built over time through honesty and consistent actions. If you feel you always have to second-guess what someone says or if you suspect they often lie, trust is weak. In a healthy bond, you can share your secrets or concerns knowing the other person will not use them against you or spread them around. Similarly, you honor their trust by keeping private information private.

3.3 Communication

Good communication goes beyond talking. It includes listening, asking questions, and clarifying to avoid misunderstandings. In a healthy relationship, people feel free to speak up about what is bothering them. They also try to explain their needs in a calm, honest manner.

3.4 Support and Encouragement

A supportive friend or partner cheers for your victories and comforts you in tough times. They do not feel threatened by your success or dismiss your problems. Even if they do not fully understand your situation, they try to be there for you in the best way they can. In return, you do the same for them.

3.5 Boundaries

Boundaries are limits that protect your sense of self. They might be emotional boundaries (like not wanting to discuss certain personal topics) or physical ones (like not wanting to be touched in certain ways). In a healthy relationship, both people respect these limits without pressuring the other to change them.

4. Recognizing Signs of Unhealthy Relationships

4.1 Control and Manipulation

Some people try to control who you hang out with, what you wear, or how you spend your time. They might use guilt or threats to get their way. This behavior is not caring; it is manipulative. If you notice these signs, it is a strong warning that the relationship may be unhealthy.

4.2 Lack of Respect

If the other person calls you names, mocks your appearance, or dismisses your opinions, they are not showing respect. Constantly cutting you off mid-sentence, ignoring your boundaries, or forcing you into activities you do not like are also signs of disrespect.

4.3 Dishonesty

Healthy relationships rely on honesty, even if the truth sometimes stings. If you catch someone in frequent lies or realize they hide things from you, trust gets damaged. Once trust is broken, it can be very hard to repair unless both sides commit to honest communication.

4.4 Intimidation or Fear

You should not feel scared of a friend, partner, or family member. If you constantly worry they will blow up in anger or punish you, that is a red flag. Healthy relationships can have disagreements, but those conflicts should not involve fear tactics or threats.

4.5 Isolation

An unhealthy partner or friend might discourage you from hanging out with others. They may want you all to themselves, making you feel guilty if you spend time with your family or other friends. Isolation can leave you with fewer people to turn to if the relationship becomes worse.

5. Communication in Relationships

5.1 Active Listening

When the other person talks, try to understand their point of view without forming a reply in your head right away. Make eye contact if you can (or at least look in their general direction), and ask follow-up questions if something is unclear. This shows respect and helps avoid misunderstandings.

5.2 Expressing Yourself Clearly

When sharing your thoughts, be as direct and calm as possible. Instead of saying, "You always ignore me," try, "I feel overlooked when I text you and don't hear back." This style of communication focuses on your feelings rather than labeling the other person's actions in a harsh way.

5.3 Handling Disagreements

Arguments happen even in the healthiest relationships. The key is to argue in a way that leads to understanding rather than deeper conflict.

- Stay respectful: No name-calling or yelling.
- Take breaks if emotions run too high: Sometimes, stepping away to cool off can prevent mean words you might regret later.
- Seek common ground: Look for a point you can both agree on, even if it is small.

5.4 Digital Communication

Texting and social media can sometimes create confusion because it is easy to misread someone's tone. If a text or post seems harsh, ask for clarification before assuming the worst. Also, remember that talking in person or by phone can resolve complex issues more effectively than texting back and forth.

6. Setting Boundaries and Knowing Your Limits

6.1 What Are Boundaries?

Boundaries are like invisible lines that define how much emotional or physical closeness you are okay with. They also cover how you want to be treated. You have the right to say "no" to things that make you uncomfortable, whether it is sharing personal details, physical affection, or certain activities.

6.2 Why Boundaries Are Important

Without boundaries, you can lose track of your own needs and feelings, trying to always please the other person. This can lead to stress, resentment, or even emotional harm. Boundaries keep relationships balanced, ensuring each person's well-being is respected.

6.3 Tips for Stating Boundaries

1. **Be Clear:** Use direct statements like "I do not like it when…" or "I need some time alone right now."
2. **Stand Firm:** If the other person tries to push you beyond your boundary, calmly repeat your stance. You do not need to argue, just restate it.
3. **Offer Alternatives (Sometimes):** If a friend wants to hang out every day, but that is too much, you might say, "I can't meet daily, but I'd be happy to catch up once or twice a week."

6.4 Respecting Others' Boundaries

Healthy relationships go both ways. Just as you deserve to have your limits respected, so do others. If a friend says they are too busy to hang out, or a partner says they are not ready for a certain step in the relationship, respect their choice. Pressuring them is not okay.

7. Romantic Relationships Basics

7.1 Emotional Readiness

Before you start dating, ask yourself if you feel emotionally ready. Are you comfortable talking about your feelings? Can you handle disagreements calmly? Are you prepared to respect someone else's boundaries and share parts of your own life? Dating when you are not prepared can lead to stress and misunderstandings.

7.2 Healthy Dating Patterns

- **Mutual Respect:** You both value each other's opinions and feelings.
- **Open Communication:** You can discuss problems or worries without fear.
- **Balance:** You do not lose your individuality or ignore your friends just because you are dating. You keep other parts of your life active.
- **No Pressure:** Neither person forces the other into physical or emotional situations they are not ready for.

7.3 Handling Breakups

Not all romantic relationships last forever. Ending a relationship can be sad or painful, but it is often a natural part of learning about what works for you. If a breakup happens, give yourself time to heal. Talk to friends or a trusted adult about your feelings rather than bottling them up. Avoid the urge to get revenge or spread rumors. A respectful ending can help both people move on in a healthier way.

---

8. Family Dynamics

8.1 Communicating with Parents or Guardians

Sometimes you might feel your parents do not understand you. They might seem strict or have different views. Being open and honest can bridge some gaps. For example, if you want more independence, explain why you think you can handle it, and suggest ways to show responsibility (like keeping track of your chores or finishing homework on time).

8.2 Sibling Relationships

If you have siblings, you might argue over shared space, time, or resources. These conflicts can be handled by setting rules you both agree on. For instance, you might schedule who uses the TV or computer at certain times. Good communication and fairness can reduce daily fights.

8.3 Handling Family Tension

Some families face bigger challenges, such as divorce, financial stress, or ongoing disagreements. You might feel caught in the middle or burdened by adult problems. It is crucial to remember you are not responsible for solving adult issues. If it becomes too much, talk to a school counselor or another trusted adult to help you cope.

---

9. Seeking Help for Relationship Problems

9.1 When to Seek Outside Support

- If someone close to you is verbally or physically harming you.
- If you suspect emotional manipulation or controlling behavior.
- If you feel isolated and have no one to talk to about your problems.
- If family conflicts or romantic issues leave you feeling constantly depressed or anxious.

9.2 Who Can Help?

- **School Counselors:** They can offer one-on-one sessions, mediate conflicts, or point you to external resources.
- **Hotlines:** In many regions, there are phone or text hotlines for teens dealing with abuse, bullying, or relationship stress.

- **Trusted Adults:** A teacher, coach, neighbor, or relative might listen and guide you. Sometimes just sharing your experience with a caring adult can help you see options you did not notice before.
- **Therapists or Community Centers:** If available, professional counselors can help you understand complex family or dating issues, teach coping strategies, and improve your communication skills.

9.3 Speaking Up

Standing up for yourself or someone else in an unhealthy situation can feel scary, but it can also protect you and others from ongoing harm. If you see a friend being mistreated by a partner or bullied by a group, encourage them to seek help or even offer to go with them to speak to a counselor.

---

10. Building Stronger Relationships

10.1 Shared Activities

Spending positive time together is one way to strengthen bonds. Whether it is playing a board game with siblings, going to a sports practice with friends, or volunteering with your partner, shared experiences create good memories and deepen understanding of each other.

10.2 Giving and Receiving Honest Feedback

In healthy relationships, you can point out when the other person could improve, and they can do the same for you—kindly. For example, if your friend often shows up late, you might say, "It bothers me when you're late because it feels like you don't value my time." If they care about the relationship, they will try to change their behavior, and you can do the same when they raise an issue.

10.3 Appreciation

Letting people know you value them can keep a relationship healthy. This could be a small note, a verbal "thank you for listening," or even a simple text saying you are happy they are in your life. It does not need to be grand or expensive. Genuine words often mean a lot.

---

11. Relationship Myths to Avoid

11.1 "We Never Fight, So It Must Be Perfect"

No disagreements at all might mean someone is afraid to speak up, not that the relationship is flawless. Occasional conflicts are natural. The key is how respectfully you handle them.

11.2 "Family Conflict Is Always Your Fault"

Young people sometimes blame themselves for family issues. In reality, many family struggles have complex roots that involve adult responsibilities or problems. You are not to blame for everything that goes wrong at home. Focus on how you respond, not taking on guilt that is not yours.

11.3 "I Can Fix Someone by Loving Them Enough"

It is common to think you can change someone's harmful habits if you just care about them a lot. However, people change when they decide to, not because you force them. If a friend or partner constantly acts hurtfully and refuses help, you cannot "fix" them by sacrificing your own well-being.

Chapter 11: Social Media and Self-Worth

1. Introduction

Social media is a major part of teen life today. You might use it to keep in touch with friends, follow trends, watch videos, or post photos. While these platforms can be fun and helpful, they can also influence how you feel about yourself. You might find yourself comparing your life to what you see online, feeling both excited and worried about how you appear to others.

This chapter looks at how social media can affect your self-worth, which is the sense of value you have for yourself. We will explore the good sides and the problematic sides, discuss how likes and comments can shape your mood, and suggest ways to keep social media from harming your confidence. By the end, you should have a clearer view of how to use social media carefully while staying true to your real self.

2. What Social Media Is and Why It Matters

2.1 Basic Definition

Social media platforms are websites or apps where people create accounts, post updates, and interact with one another. Examples include Instagram, TikTok, Snapchat, and many others. You might share pictures, write short messages, or post stories about your day. These platforms often have features like "likes," comments, or reactions that show how people respond to your posts.

2.2 The Role of Connection

The main point of social media is to connect people. For teens, it offers ways to interact with friends outside of school, follow influencers or public figures, and discover new interests. If you like reading, for example, you might find online groups that talk about books. This connectivity can help you feel less alone, especially if you have a niche hobby or want to share creative works.

2.3 Why It Can Affect Self-Worth

When you share parts of your life online, you often receive instant feedback. If you get a lot of likes or encouraging comments, you may feel good. But if your post does not get much attention, or if you receive unkind remarks, it might lower your mood. Over time, you might come to depend on this feedback to measure your value. This can create a cycle where your sense of self hinges on how many people respond positively to what you post.

---

3. Positive Aspects of Social Media for Teen Girls

3.1 Finding Community and Support

One of the main upsides of social media is the chance to meet people who share your interests or experiences. For instance, if you are passionate about art, you can follow artists who inspire you. You might even post your own work and get constructive feedback. Similarly, if you are going through a tough time—such as dealing with an illness or feeling isolated—you can find support groups or hashtags that connect you with others who understand.

3.2 Learning New Things

Social media can expose you to new knowledge and skills. You can watch short tutorials on cooking, painting, or learning a language. Many experts and educators share useful tips or short lessons. If you follow credible accounts, you can expand your learning outside of school in a fun, quick way.

3.3 Building Friendships

Some friendships start or grow stronger through social media. You might find someone who goes to the same school but whom you have never talked to in person. Online interaction can break the ice, leading to face-to-face connections later. Also, if you have friends who moved away, social media provides a convenient way to stay in touch.

3.4 Showcasing Talents

Platforms like TikTok or Instagram let you share your singing, dancing, artwork, or writing. This can boost your confidence if you receive encouraging feedback. Showcasing your abilities online can also help you track your progress over time. Plus, you might inspire others who see your posts and realize they can also try those activities.

---

4. Potential Drawbacks and Dangers

4.1 Comparison with Others

One of the biggest pitfalls is the habit of comparing your life to the curated images you see on your feed. People usually post their best moments—like vacation pictures, new clothes, or achievements. You rarely see everyday struggles or negative moments. This can create the impression that everyone else is living an amazing life while you deal with daily stress. If you compare their highlight reel to your normal reality, you may feel inadequate.

4.2 Cyberbullying

Social media can also be a place where bullying occurs. Cyberbullying might come in the form of hurtful comments, teasing, or rumors spread online. Because it happens on the internet, it can follow you home in a way that traditional bullying might not. This can harm your self-esteem and make you dread checking your phone.

4.3 Privacy Issues

Many teens share personal details on social media. Some post photos that reveal their school, neighborhood, or other personal info. This can lead to safety risks if strangers gain access to that information. Even if you trust your followers, there is always a chance that a screenshot or forwarded post can spread far beyond your intended audience.

4.4 Unrealistic Beauty and Lifestyle Standards

Filters, photo editing apps, and carefully staged pictures can set impossible standards for looks or lifestyles. You might feel pressure to appear perfect, whether that means always wearing stylish outfits or hiding any imperfections. Over time, this pressure can result in anxiety, body dissatisfaction, or a sense that you are never "enough."

---

5. How Social Media Affects Self-Worth

5.1 The "Like" Culture

Many platforms display likes or hearts as a measure of how people respond to your posts. Seeing these numbers can feel like a direct measure of your popularity or attractiveness. Some teens might start deleting posts if they do not get enough likes, believing that low engagement reflects poorly on them. This can make your self-esteem dependent on external approval, which is fragile and ever-changing.

5.2 FOMO (Fear of Missing Out)

Scrolling through posts where your friends are at a party, on a trip, or simply hanging out without you can lead to FOMO. You might wonder why you were not invited or worry you are not part of the "cool" crowd. This fear can make you anxious or lonely, even if you have plenty of positives in your own life.

5.3 Shift in Focus

Constant use of social media can pull your attention away from real-life goals and relationships. Instead of focusing on what you enjoy doing—like hobbies or spending time with family—you might become fixated on posting the "perfect shot" or checking notifications. This shift can erode your sense of self if you begin to see your life mainly through how it appears online.

5.4 Emotional Ups and Downs

Social media amplifies emotional swings. A kind comment can make your day, while a mean message can ruin it. Over time, these swings can make it hard to maintain a stable sense of self-worth. You might develop a habit of checking your phone constantly to see if there is any new feedback that will either lift your mood or bring it down.

6. Recognizing When Social Media Lowers Your Confidence

6.1 Feeling Anxious or Depressed After Checking Your Feed

If you consistently feel worse about yourself or your life after browsing social media, it might be a sign that it is affecting your self-worth negatively. Pay attention to your emotions. Do you feel jealous, sad, or irritated? This awareness is the first step toward making changes.

6.2 Obsessed with Likes and Comments

If you cannot stop refreshing your feed to see how many likes you got, or if a small dip in likes ruins your day, it might be time to step back. Real-life worth is not measured by numbers on a screen, and chasing these metrics can become addictive.

6.3 Changing Your Behavior to Fit an Online Image

Some teens find themselves dressing differently, speaking differently, or engaging in activities they do not actually enjoy just to look appealing on social media. If you notice you are altering your genuine self just for online approval, it could point to a deeper issue with self-esteem.

6.4 Frequent Feelings of Envy

Social media can create strong envy or bitterness if you are constantly seeing posts of others having fun, wearing trendy clothes, or showing off new items. While envy is a normal emotion once in a while, feeling it frequently might indicate an unhealthy reliance on social media images to gauge your own worth.

---

7. Strategies for Healthy Social Media Use

7.1 Set Time Limits

It is easy to get lost in endless scrolling. Consider using apps or phone settings that limit how long you can be on certain platforms each day. Even taking short breaks—like a weekend without social media—can help you refocus on your offline life.

7.2 Curate Your Feed

Look at who you follow. Do they consistently make you feel inspired or do they trigger self-doubt? If certain accounts spark negative thoughts, it is okay to unfollow or mute them. Choose accounts that align with your interests, positivity, or genuine learning experiences.

7.3 Engage, Do Not Just Scroll

Instead of passively looking at posts, actively connect with people who support you. Comment something kind on a friend's post, join a constructive group discussion, or share useful resources. Shifting from passive consumption to positive engagement can make social media more meaningful.

7.4 Balance Online and Offline Activities

Make sure your day includes plenty of offline moments—like spending time with friends face to face, going for a walk, reading a book, or practicing a hobby. These offline pursuits can remind you that your value does not depend on internet validation.

---

8. Dealing with Negative Interactions

8.1 Handling Hurtful Comments

If someone leaves a mean comment on your post, respond wisely. Sometimes ignoring or blocking is the best route, particularly if the comment is rude or bullying. If it is someone you know, you could politely ask them to clarify why they said that. If they continue to be unkind, stepping away from the interaction is usually the healthier choice. You are not obligated to keep engaging with negativity.

8.2 Cyberbullying Steps

- **Document Everything:** Take screenshots of hurtful messages or profiles.
- **Tell an Adult You Trust:** A counselor, teacher, or parent can guide you and help you decide on the next steps.
- **Block the Person:** Use the platform's block feature so they cannot reach you as easily.
- **Report the Activity:** Most social media platforms have a way to report harassment. Use it if someone is targeting you repeatedly.

8.3 Not Feeding the Trolls

The term "trolls" often refers to people who deliberately post inflammatory comments to spark arguments. Engaging with them can lead to stress and more negative remarks. If you suspect someone is trying to provoke you or cause a scene, the best response might be no response at all.

---

9. Building Realistic Self-Worth

9.1 Focus on Personal Achievements

Make a list of things you have accomplished, whether big or small. Maybe you improved in a certain subject, picked up a new skill, or helped a friend. These achievements are meaningful, even if they did not get many "likes" online. Recognizing your real-life successes helps you see that your value goes beyond an app.

9.2 Keep Perspective

Remember that a social media profile is just a slice of someone's reality. People choose what to show and often only display the best parts. If you find yourself comparing your entire life to someone's highlight reel, remind yourself you are seeing a curated version of their existence.

9.3 Practice Mindful Self-Talk

When you catch yourself thinking, "Why is my life so boring compared to theirs?" replace that thought with something more balanced like, "I don't see the boring parts of their life. I have good moments too." This switch can prevent negative thoughts from dominating your mind.

9.4 Seek Offline Approval

Relying on online metrics can be risky because they are fleeting and influenced by algorithms, timing, or luck. Instead, value offline connections. Notice when friends or family compliment you or show appreciation. Their supportive words are more stable signs of genuine connection than a random number of likes.

10. Balancing Creativity and Authenticity Online

10.1 Sharing Your True Passions

If you love drawing, playing music, or writing, post about those interests in a way that reflects your genuine style. You do not have to mold your art to match popular trends if that is not what truly speaks to you. The more authentic you are, the more likely you are to attract people who genuinely resonate with you.

10.2 Keeping Some Things Private

Not everything needs to be posted. Certain memories might hold more meaning if you keep them within a close circle of friends or family, rather than broadcasting them to the internet. Saving some experiences for yourself helps maintain a boundary between your personal life and your online persona.

10.3 Avoiding Perfectionism

Do not feel you must only post flawless moments or polished photos. If you want to share a goofy picture or a day when things did not go right, that can show authenticity. People often connect with realness more than they do with an obviously staged image.

11. When to Take a Break or Seek Help

11.1 Signs You Need a Digital Detox

- You feel anxious if you cannot check your phone for a short time.
- You constantly compare your life to others.

- You experience sleeplessness or trouble focusing on schoolwork because you are always scrolling.
- Social media arguments or unkind comments keep you stressed.

If these issues sound familiar, consider logging out for a set period—like a weekend or a week—to see if your mood improves.

11.2 Talking to Friends or Adults

If you notice social media is harming your self-confidence, talk about it. Friends might share similar feelings, and you can decide as a group to spend less time online or to support each other with positive comments. If the problem feels serious, consider talking to a school counselor or a trusted adult about how to handle online stress.

11.3 Professional Help

In some cases, social media triggers deeper issues like anxiety, depression, or eating disorders (in response to idealized body images). If you find yourself struggling with serious emotional distress, it might help to see a mental health professional. This does not mean you are weak. On the contrary, seeking help shows you care enough about your health to look for solutions.

---

12. Real-Life Scenarios

12.1 Jade's Experience with Instagram

Jade used to spend hours each day browsing fashion influencers. She began feeling inferior because her wardrobe was smaller and her daily life seemed plain compared to their glamorous posts. One day, she decided to unfollow several accounts that made her feel bad. She replaced them with positive pages about affordable fashion and creative re-styling. Over time, her self-esteem improved, and she found greater enjoyment in expressing her personal style without feeling pressured to match high-end looks.

12.2 Noah's Struggle with Negative Comments

Noah liked to share short singing videos on TikTok. Most people were supportive, but one user wrote mean comments about his voice, calling him names. At first, Noah tried to argue back, but it only led to more hurtful replies. He finally blocked the user and reported them. He also talked to his older sister, who reminded him that many great singers face criticism online. With a renewed focus on improving his skills, Noah continued posting songs and felt better ignoring the trolls.

12.3 Lily's Time Limit Approach

Lily realized she was missing out on real-life moments because she was always checking her phone. She started by setting a daily limit of one hour for social media apps using a built-in timer on her phone. After a few days, she noticed she felt calmer and more present when chatting with her family or hanging out with friends. She even rediscovered her love for playing board games with her younger brother, something she had not done in ages.

Chapter 12: Overcoming Criticism

1. Introduction

Criticism is feedback that points out errors, weaknesses, or areas for improvement. While it can be a helpful tool for learning and growing, it can also hurt. Teen girls, in particular, may face criticism about everything from school performance to appearance. At times, criticism can come from friends, family, teachers, or even strangers online. Learning to handle it calmly and productively is a key step in building confidence.

In this chapter, we will explore different types of criticism—both the kind that can help you and the kind meant to tear you down. We will look at why some people criticize, how to figure out if the critique is fair, and ways to respond without harming your self-esteem. By the end, you should have strategies to face criticism in a way that leads to personal growth rather than self-doubt.

2. Types of Criticism

2.1 Constructive Criticism

This type of feedback is meant to help you do better. For example, a teacher might say, "Your essay has good ideas, but the introduction needs to be clearer. Think about starting with a strong statement." Here, the criticism is specific, focuses on a changeable part of your work, and offers guidance on how to improve. Constructive criticism usually comes from someone who has your best interests in mind.

2.2 Destructive Criticism

Destructive criticism aims to tear you down or express negativity without offering a path for improvement. It might involve insults, blame, or disrespectful language. For example, if someone says, "Your artwork is dumb; you have no talent," there is nothing in that comment that helps you learn. This type of criticism often reflects the critic's own insecurities more than any real flaw in you.

2.3 Internal Criticism (Self-Criticism)

Sometimes the harshest critic is in your own mind. You might blame yourself for small mistakes or assume you are inadequate before anyone else even weighs in. This inner voice can be helpful if it points out areas you can fix, but it can become harmful if it constantly puts you down and lowers your self-confidence.

2.4 Group Criticism

Certain situations involve multiple people offering feedback—like a group critique in a music class or a peer-review session in writing class. Group criticism can feel intense because you receive comments from many directions at once. Learning to sort through these comments to find what is truly helpful is an important skill.

---

3. Why People Criticize

3.1 Genuine Concern

Some critics genuinely care about your growth. A parent might point out that you are not studying enough because they want you to succeed academically. A coach might say your posture is off in a dance routine so you can correct it and perform better. While the words might sting, the intention is positive.

3.2 Personal Insecurity

Other times, people criticize to feel better about themselves. Maybe a classmate feels anxious about her own looks, so she picks on your outfit to deflect attention. Criticism rooted in insecurity often lacks substance and focuses on shallow or irrelevant details.

3.3 Lack of Empathy

Some critics just do not know how to share feedback in a kind way. They might mean well but come across as harsh because they lack empathy or social skills. Understanding that the issue might be their communication style can help you not take every harsh word to heart.

3.4 Desire to Control

In certain cases, destructive criticism is used to control or manipulate. A friend or partner might criticize you to diminish your self-esteem, making you rely on their approval. If you suspect the critique is part of a controlling pattern, it may signal an unhealthy relationship.

---

4. How Criticism Affects Confidence

4.1 Emotional Impact

Words have power. A negative remark from a person you respect can make you question your abilities. Over time, repeated criticism without balance can erode your self-esteem. You might stop trying new activities because you fear more negative feedback.

4.2 Doubting Your Abilities

When you are criticized harshly, you might doubt skills you once felt comfortable with. For instance, if you always loved singing but a teacher's strict critique makes you feel untalented, you might begin avoiding music altogether. This doubt can spread, making you hesitate to try other things as well.

4.3 Behavior Changes

Persistent criticism might cause you to shift how you act, talk, or dress in an effort to avoid remarks. While making certain adjustments can be beneficial—for example, improving your study habits—changing your core identity just to dodge disapproval is not healthy. This can leave you feeling disconnected from who you truly are.

4.4 Internalizing Negativity

Sometimes, you start repeating the critic's words in your own mind. Even when the critic is not around, you may catch yourself saying, "I'm no good at this" or "I'm unworthy." This is an example of internalizing negativity, where external criticism becomes part of your own self-image.

---

5. Assessing the Criticism

5.1 Ask: Is It True?

Not all criticism is accurate. Sometimes, people misunderstand or have incomplete information. If someone says, "You never pay attention in class," but you know you do—except for a few days you were exhausted—then the statement might be an overgeneralization. Try to see if any part of the critique holds truth or if it is an exaggeration.

5.2 Ask: Is It Specific?

Useful feedback often points to a specific area you can improve. Vague comments like, "You're bad at sports," do not help. If a critique is too broad or lacks clear examples, it might not be worth taking to heart. On the other hand, if someone says, "Your tennis serve is inconsistent because of your grip," you have something concrete to work on.

5.3 Consider the Source

Who is offering the criticism? If it is a teacher with expertise in the subject, their input might be more credible. If it is a random peer who often speaks negatively about others, perhaps you can place less weight on their opinions. Also, think about how well they know you. A close friend who sees your daily habits might offer more accurate observations than someone who barely interacts with you.

5.4 Look at the Intention

Try to sense if the critic is genuinely aiming to help or just wanting to hurt you. This can be tricky, but tone and context matter. If the person is calm, offers suggestions, and seems open to discussion, the feedback is likely constructive. If they are rude, mocking, or refusing to clarify, they might just want to put you down.

---

6. Strategies to Handle Criticism Calmly

6.1 Pause Before Reacting

When you first hear a critical remark, you might feel a rush of emotions—anger, embarrassment, or sadness. Take a brief moment to breathe. Count to three in your head, or practice a quick breathing exercise. This short pause can prevent you from reacting impulsively.

6.2 Ask for Clarification

If the critique is unclear, ask polite questions. "Can you give an example of what you mean?" or "Which part did you find confusing?" show that you are willing to learn more about their point. If the critic does not have a clear answer, it might indicate the criticism is not well-founded.

6.3 Acknowledge Valid Points

If part of the criticism is fair, acknowledge it. You can say something like, "I see what you're saying about my introduction being weak. I'll work on that." Accepting valid feedback shows maturity and openness to improvement. At the same time, you do not have to accept the entire critique if some parts feel off base.

6.4 Offer Your Perspective

Sometimes, critics do not see the full picture. After listening, you can calmly explain your side. For instance, "I appreciate your advice on my presentation. I was actually sick that day, which affected my voice." This helps the critic understand your situation and might lead to a more balanced view.

---

7. Responding to Destructive Criticism

7.1 Do Not Engage in a Fight

When someone aims to hurt you with words, replying with anger often escalates the conflict. If possible, keep your response short or ignore it. Fueling a heated argument can give the critic more reason to continue. Sometimes silence or a simple, "I disagree," is enough to show you will not be provoked.

7.2 Set Boundaries

If a person repeatedly tears you down, let them know it is not acceptable. You could say, "I understand you have an opinion, but I won't allow you to insult me." If they persist, distance yourself or seek help from a teacher, counselor, or another authority figure if this happens in a school context. You have the right to protect your mental and emotional well-being.

7.3 Seek Support

Sharing your experience with friends, family, or a mentor can help you process destructive remarks. They might reassure you that the criticism is unfounded or give you pointers on how to handle it in the future. Talking it out also prevents the negativity from lingering in your mind.

7.4 Remember Their Opinion Is Not a Fact

Destructive criticism is often based on personal bias rather than objective truth. Keep in mind that one person's mean comment does not define you. Who you are is shaped by your experiences, values, skills, and the positive traits you bring into the world—not by an insult.

---

8. Turning Criticism into Growth

8.1 Embrace the Lesson

Try to find something you can learn, even from harsh feedback. For example, if a teacher's tone is strict but they say you need clearer paragraphs in your paper, focus on what you can do to improve your writing. Let the negative tone pass, and pick out the helpful tip.

8.2 Keep a Growth Mindset

A growth-focused outlook tells you that you can develop skills with effort. If the critique points out a weakness, you can see it as a reminder that everyone has areas they can strengthen. This perspective helps you feel less threatened by criticism and more driven to do better.

8.3 Track Your Progress

If you receive recurring feedback—like that your singing pitch is off—start tracking your improvement over time. Practice regularly, maybe record yourself, and note the changes. When you see real growth, it can counter any earlier negative remarks, showing that you are capable of positive change.

8.4 Evaluate Feedback Over Time

Some advice might not make sense when you first hear it, but could be more relevant later. For instance, a mentor might say, "Learn to manage your time better," and you do not see the importance until you face a busy schedule. Keep a mental or written note of repeated critiques, then revisit them when you are ready to grow in that area.

9. Handling Self-Criticism

9.1 Identifying Negative Self-Talk

Listen to your internal dialogue. Do you often say, "I'm not smart enough" or "I'm always messing up"? These thoughts can feel automatic, but they are learned habits. Recognizing them as negative self-talk is the first step in changing them.

9.2 Challenge the Inner Critic

Ask yourself if your negative thoughts are based on facts or assumptions. If you got one math question wrong, it does not mean you are "terrible at math." Replace that thought with, "I made a mistake this time, but I can learn from it." This reframing helps break the cycle of self-blame.

9.3 Practicing Compassion Toward Yourself

Think of how you would respond to a close friend who feels down. You would likely reassure them and point out their good qualities. Offer yourself the same kindness. For instance, after a disappointment, remind yourself of your past successes or times you overcame problems.

9.4 Setting Realistic Expectations

High standards can fuel harsh self-criticism. If you demand perfection in every project, you set yourself up for constant dissatisfaction. Aim for growth rather than flawlessness. Knowing it is okay to make errors can lower internal pressure and keep you from tearing yourself down each time.

---

10. Coping Tools and Exercises

10.1 Write It Out

If someone criticizes you in a way that bothers you, try journaling about the experience. Write down what was said, how it made you feel, and what parts (if any) might be helpful. This process can bring clarity and reduce emotional clutter.

10.2 Role-Play with a Friend

If you are nervous about facing future criticism, ask a friend to practice with you. Let them pretend to offer feedback (constructive or harsh), and work on responding calmly. Hearing critical words from someone you trust can lower your fear of real-life confrontation.

10.3 The "Compliment Collection"

Keep a small box, notebook, or digital folder with positive comments you have received from teachers, family, or friends. On days when criticism weighs heavily on you, look through these compliments. They can balance out the negative remarks and remind you of your strengths.

10.4 Meditation or Mindfulness

Spending even a few minutes each day in quiet reflection or simple mindful breathing can help you handle stress better. By learning to calm your mind, you are less likely to react sharply to criticism. You can process the words more rationally and decide how to respond.

11. Real-Life Examples

11.1 Nina's Dance Class

Nina joined a dance class where the instructor was known for tough feedback. Initially, Nina felt hurt when the instructor pointed out her mistakes. But she tried to pick out the useful parts of the criticism: improving her posture and timing. Over time, she not only got better at dancing but also grew more comfortable hearing pointed feedback, since she saw it paid off in her progress.

11.2 Eli and His Best Friend

Eli's best friend often made little jokes about Eli's fashion choices, calling them "too plain." At first, Eli laughed along, but he eventually realized these comments were affecting his self-esteem. He told his friend calmly, "I know you are joking, but it hurts when you knock my style. I like dressing this way." His friend apologized, and the jokes stopped. Eli felt relieved and learned the importance of speaking up.

11.3 Tia's Magazine Article

Tia wrote an article for her school magazine. The editorial team returned it with lots of red marks and notes to rewrite certain paragraphs. Tia felt discouraged, thinking she was a poor writer. However, after carefully reading the comments, she saw they were actually giving her tips to tighten her arguments and use clearer words. Once she made those changes, the piece turned out much stronger, and she felt proud when it was published.

Chapter 13: The Power of Positive Role Models

1. Introduction

A positive role model is someone you look up to—someone who shows you what is possible and encourages you to become your best self. Role models can be family members, teachers, friends, celebrities, historical figures, or even fictional characters. The main idea is that they have qualities you admire, such as kindness, determination, creativity, or bravery.

Many teen girls find it helpful to have at least one person they see as an example of good character and achievement. This does not mean you must copy everything they do. Instead, you watch how they handle stress, how they treat others, or how they stay true to their values. You can learn from their approaches and adapt them to your own life.

This chapter explores how to identify truly positive role models, the benefits and potential pitfalls of looking up to certain people, and how you can become your own role model as you gain confidence. By the end, you should have a clearer idea of how to pick the right influences and use their example to grow in healthy ways.

2. What Is a Role Model?

2.1 Basic Definition

A role model is someone you respect or admire for their qualities or achievements. You might like how they give back to the community, how they handle challenges, or how they pursue their goals. This admiration can guide your actions, whether consciously or unconsciously.

2.2 Different Types of Role Models

1. **Close Circle Role Models:** This includes family, friends, or teachers you know in real life. You see these people often, which allows you to observe their behavior up close and ask them questions.
2. **Public Figures or Celebrities:** These can be singers, actors, athletes, or influencers. You may not know them personally, but their stories, interviews, or work can inspire you.
3. **Historical Role Models:** Sometimes, people from the past—leaders, inventors, activists—can show courage or creativity in ways that motivate you. Reading about them can give you insights into resilience and success.
4. **Fictional Characters:** A character in a book, movie, or show might have traits you want to develop. While fictional, their experiences can still offer lessons in kindness, perseverance, or empathy.

2.3 Why Role Models Matter

Role models serve as examples of what is possible. If you see someone from a similar background who reached a big achievement, you might think, "If they could do it, maybe I can too." This can push you to dream bigger or keep going when obstacles show up. Additionally, role models can help shape your sense of right and wrong, encouraging values like honesty, generosity, and respect.

---

3. Characteristics of a Positive Role Model

3.1 Integrity

Integrity means doing the right thing, even when no one is watching. A positive role model's words match their actions. They do not pretend to have one set of morals and then do something completely different behind the scenes. This consistency can teach you the value of honesty and the strength it takes to stay true to your values.

3.2 Resilience

Resilience is the ability to recover from failures or hardships. A good role model does not necessarily have a perfect life; instead, they face setbacks with courage and a willingness to keep trying. Watching them handle difficulties can inspire you to see problems as challenges to work through rather than reasons to give up.

3.3 Compassion

Someone who cares about others and shows empathy can be a powerful influence. They might volunteer in their community, stand up for someone who is being treated unfairly, or simply lend an ear to a friend in need. Observing compassionate actions can make you more considerate and open-hearted.

3.4 Goal-Focused

A role model often sets meaningful goals and works steadily toward them. They have discipline and a clear sense of what they want to accomplish. This can help you see the importance of planning, persistence, and self-motivation. It also shows that real success usually results from consistent effort rather than instant luck.

3.5 Humility

Even if a role model is highly skilled or well-known, they remain respectful and do not act superior. They recognize their strengths without belittling others. This humility can teach you that confidence does not require looking down on people or boasting about your achievements.

---

4. Benefits of Having a Positive Role Model

4.1 Inspiration to Aim Higher

When you watch someone you admire, you may see them accomplishing things you once thought were out of reach. For example, if your role model is a female scientist, her work could inspire you to look into STEM fields. Knowing someone like you has succeeded can motivate you to set bigger goals.

4.2 Guidance Through Challenges

Role models can offer both direct and indirect advice. If you know them personally, you might ask them how they managed certain issues. If they are a public figure, reading about their life or listening to their speeches can give you ideas on handling obstacles. Their examples become a blueprint for how to act under pressure.

4.3 Reinforcement of Good Values

Seeing someone consistently display traits like honesty, kindness, or responsibility can strengthen your commitment to those qualities. Role models show that being good-hearted or working ethically pays off, even if the path is not the easiest in the moment.

4.4 Personal Growth

By looking up to a role model, you can discover more about your own strengths and weaknesses. If you notice they are very organized and you are not, you might try to improve in that area. If they speak confidently, you might practice speaking clearly. This growth can build your confidence as you expand your skill set.

---

5. Potential Pitfalls in Choosing Role Models

5.1 Overlooking Human Flaws

Even admirable people have shortcomings. If you see your role model as perfect, you may feel betrayed if you find out they made a mistake or have a hidden habit you do not approve of. It is important to remember that role models are human and can make errors. This does not necessarily cancel out the good things they have done, but it is a reminder to avoid blindly idolizing anyone.

5.2 Misleading Public Images

Some public figures present a polished image that might not reflect who they really are. Celebrities on social media might appear extremely generous or successful while actually dealing with personal problems behind closed doors. Relying too heavily on curated public images can lead to unrealistic expectations for yourself and others.

5.3 Negative Influences

Not every well-known person is a good role model. Some celebrities might have problematic behaviors—like encouraging harmful habits, speaking disrespectfully, or breaking the law. If you choose someone with these traits as a role model, you might end up normalizing bad behavior or adopting unhealthy values.

5.4 Pressure to Compare

Sometimes, looking up to a very successful person can make you feel inadequate if you start comparing your life to theirs. You might think, "I can never reach that level," which can harm your self-esteem. A healthy approach is to appreciate your role model's achievements as motivation rather than a reason to feel inferior.

---

6. Finding the Right Role Models

6.1 Look for Genuine Qualities

Focus on traits that really matter to you—such as compassion, perseverance, creativity, or confidence. Check if your potential role model consistently demonstrates these traits. You can watch interviews, read articles, or observe them in person if possible.

6.2 Diversify Your Influences

Having more than one role model can be helpful. Maybe one inspires your athletic side, another sparks your interest in art, and a third guides you in leadership or community service. By drawing from multiple sources, you get a broader perspective and avoid putting one person on too high a pedestal.

6.3 Consider Local Role Models

Sometimes, the best influences are closer than you think. A neighbor who volunteers every weekend, a teacher who stays after class to help students, or an older cousin who overcame life challenges might all be great examples. Because they are part of your everyday environment, you can learn more directly from their experiences and possibly ask for advice.

6.4 Evaluate Public Figures Wisely

If you look up to a celebrity, try to go beyond their social media posts. Read interviews or watch documentaries about their real-life journey and obstacles. Notice how they treat people in various situations, not just on stage. This can help you decide whether they are the kind of influence you truly want.

---

7. Learning from Role Models

7.1 Observing Their Behavior

If your role model is someone you see regularly, pay attention to how they handle conflicts, how they speak to others, and how they plan their days. Small details can reveal bigger lessons. For instance, noticing that your older sister wakes up early to exercise might teach you about discipline and how it improves her mood.

7.2 Emulating Specific Habits

If you see a good habit, try adopting it. Perhaps your teacher credits her success to writing daily to-do lists. You might experiment with doing the same and see if it helps you stay organized. Remember, you do not need to imitate everything—just pick what aligns with your goals and values.

7.3 Asking Questions

If you have the chance to speak with your role model, do not be shy about asking for advice. You might ask, "How did you stay motivated when things got tough?" or "What daily routines help you manage stress?" Most positive role models enjoy sharing tips with people who genuinely want to grow.

7.4 Reflecting and Adapting

Finally, think about which lessons make sense for your own life. Your role model's approach to studying might not fit your schedule perfectly, or their style of communicating might feel unnatural to you. Adapt their strategies in a way that feels genuine. For example, if your role model meditates for an hour but that is too long for you, try five or ten minutes.

---

8. Becoming Your Own Role Model

8.1 Why It Matters

Depending on external role models is fine, but ultimately, you have to live with yourself 24/7. Learning to appreciate your own good qualities and actively improving the areas you are weak in can turn you into the main role model in your life. This fosters deep self-respect.

8.2 Self-Reflection

Ask yourself questions like, "What traits do I admire in others? Do I have these traits already, or can I develop them?" Think about times you faced a challenge and overcame it—what did you learn from that? Recognizing your past successes can help you see that you have qualities worth respecting.

8.3 Setting Personal Standards

A positive role model lives by certain principles. Decide what values are important to you—honesty, determination, empathy, creativity, or something else—and commit to them. When you catch yourself drifting away from these standards, gently correct course. Over time, living by your chosen values will strengthen your sense of integrity.

8.4 Celebrating Growth

A healthy kind of self-acknowledgment is noticing when you do something well or grow in a particular area. For example, if you used to procrastinate a lot but have steadily improved your study habits, remind yourself that you are capable of positive change. Recognizing these moments helps anchor your self-esteem in real progress, making you less reliant on external praise.

---

9. Balancing Admiration and Realism

9.1 Accepting Imperfections

Every human, including your favorite role model, has flaws. Admitting this fact can prevent you from feeling disappointed if they slip up. You can admire their strengths while acknowledging they are not perfect. This also reminds you that you can make mistakes and still be worthy of respect.

9.2 Avoiding Blind Imitation

Some habits might work for your role model but might not suit you at all. For instance, if they are a morning person who exercises at 5 AM, but you learn better in the evening, do not force yourself to mirror their schedule. Take the essence of what makes them successful—like consistent dedication—and adapt it to your own routine.

9.3 Being Cautious with Media Portrayals

If your role model is a public figure, be aware that interviews, photos, or documentaries can be edited to create a certain image. Do your best to find reputable sources if you really want to understand their life story. It is fine to admire their on-screen talent or accomplishments, but keep in mind that real-life complexities might not always show up in the media.

9.4 Self-Comparison vs. Self-Improvement

It is normal to compare yourself to others sometimes, but try not to let it turn into constant self-criticism. Instead, see if you can use the comparison to spark your own self-improvement. For example, "She is so confident speaking in front of the class. Maybe I can practice small presentations at home to get better at it." Focus on actionable steps rather than feeling envy or shame.

---

10. Handling Disappointment in a Role Model

10.1 Common Reasons for Disappointment

- **Discovering a Hidden Flaw:** You learn something troubling about your role model's behavior or choices.
- **Public Scandals:** A celebrity might be involved in a controversy that changes how you view them.
- **Personal Betrayal:** Someone close to you, like a mentor or coach, might act unkindly or let you down.

10.2 Emotional Impact

It can feel confusing or painful when someone you admire does something against your values. You may feel betrayed, sad, or even angry. These emotions are normal. You invested a part of your self-esteem in that person's image, so it can hurt to see them in a different light.

10.3 Finding the Lessons

If this happens, try to see if there is something to learn from it. Perhaps you realize that putting anyone on a pedestal is risky. Or you discover that you should appreciate specific behaviors or achievements rather than the person as a flawless figure. You might still respect the good they accomplished while understanding they are a complex human being.

10.4 Moving Forward

You do not necessarily have to cut off all admiration unless the behavior goes against your core values. It could be that your role model made a single mistake or has a side you were unaware of. Decide whether you can separate their positive contributions from their negative actions. If not, it may be time to find new influences that align better with who you want to be.

---

11. Encouraging Others Through Your Example

11.1 Paying It Forward

As you grow, you may find younger classmates or peers looking up to you. You do not have to be a celebrity to be someone's role model. Simply treating them with kindness, helping them study, or sharing advice can make a big impact. The positivity you show can have a ripple effect, inspiring them to help others, too.

11.2 Supporting Younger Siblings

If you have younger siblings or cousins, they often watch everything you do. By showing good habits—like reading instead of playing on your phone all day, or calmly discussing disagreements rather than shouting—you influence how they might behave. This sense of responsibility can motivate you to be more consistent in your actions.

11.3 Community Involvement

Taking part in community projects, such as local clean-ups or charity drives, can set a strong example for those around you. Even on social media, if you share genuine experiences of volunteering or learning new skills, you might become a source of motivation for your friends and followers.

11.4 Leading by Example

You do not have to give speeches about your values; actions often speak louder than words. If you are polite, punctual, and do your share of group work in class, others may notice and follow suit. This quiet leadership can be just as powerful as vocal activism.

---

12. Real-Life Stories of Role Models

12.1 Marie, the High School Mentor

Marie was a senior who excelled in math and science. She noticed that many ninth graders struggled with algebra, so she started an informal study group after school. She would patiently show them different ways to solve problems, and when they felt discouraged, she reassured them that mistakes are part of learning. Over time, Marie became a role model for younger students who saw that a strong, caring older student was on their side. They admired her not only for her math skills, but for her generosity and calm approach.

12.2 Ebony, the Local Volunteer

Ebony lived in a neighborhood with limited community resources. Instead of complaining, she organized small events, like toy drives around the holidays and a weekend reading club for elementary students. She also reached out to local businesses for donations to improve the neighborhood park. People in her community saw Ebony's can-do spirit and admired her ability to unite different groups for a common cause. She became a local role model, proving that you do not need fame or a big budget to make a difference where you live.

12.3 Sam, the College First-Generation Student

Sam's parents did not attend college, and money was tight. Despite this, he worked hard, applied for scholarships, and was accepted into a good university. He often posted tips on social media about filling out financial aid forms or searching for scholarships, hoping other teens in similar situations would not feel lost. Over time, classmates began to see Sam as someone who overcame challenges with both grit and resourcefulness. They sought his advice on everything from campus visits to managing part-time jobs, and he became a role model for breaking barriers.

---

13. Practical Exercises

13.1 Role Model Reflection

1. **List your top three role models:** They can be people you know or public figures.
2. **Identify key traits:** Under each name, note two or three qualities that stand out.
3. **Check for alignment:** Ask yourself if these qualities match your own goals and values.
4. **Plan next steps:** Choose one trait from each that you want to develop in your life. Write down an action you can take to grow in that trait.

13.2 Role Model Interview

If you have a close relationship with someone you admire, consider asking for a short interview. Prepare a few questions about their background, challenges, and tips for success. You might write these down, record them on your phone, or just have a casual conversation. Reflect on how their insights might guide your own path.

13.3 Self-Modeling Journal

Try keeping a small journal where you track moments when you behaved in a way you would admire in another person. For example, if you kindly helped a friend who was upset or if you spoke up for someone being teased, write it down. Over time, you will have a record of times you showed the qualities of a good role model to yourself. This can boost your self-esteem and encourage you to continue such behaviors.

13.4 Media Analysis

Pick a celebrity or influencer you follow. Spend a few minutes researching beyond their social media feed. Look up interviews, articles, or events they have participated in. Ask yourself if their real-life actions align with the positive image you see online. Are they consistent with values you respect, or do they promote unhealthy ideas? This process can help you decide if they deserve to remain a role model for you.

Chapter 14: Time Management

1. Introduction

Time management is the skill of organizing your tasks and activities so you can be efficient and less stressed. It is particularly important for teen girls who might be balancing school assignments, extracurricular activities, friendships, and maybe even part-time jobs. When you are short on time and have a bunch of responsibilities, it is easy to feel overwhelmed. Poor time management can leave you rushing to finish homework late at night or missing important deadlines.

This chapter explores the basics of time management: how to plan your day, prioritize your tasks, and avoid common traps like procrastination. We will also discuss how good time management relates to confidence—being on top of your schedule can make you feel more in control and capable. By the end, you should have practical tools and tips to handle your commitments more effectively, leading to a calmer mind and better results in the long run.

2. Why Time Management Matters for Confidence

2.1 Reduced Stress

When you plan your tasks, you are less likely to be surprised by last-minute deadlines. Fewer surprises often mean less anxiety. Instead of scrambling to finish everything at once, you can handle your responsibilities in manageable parts. Feeling more in control eases stress and helps you approach challenges calmly.

2.2 Better Performance

Whether it is homework, a creative project, or a sports practice, having a structured plan lets you put in consistent effort rather than cramming. This often leads to higher-quality work. As you see improvements in your grades or in your performance on the field, your confidence in your abilities grows.

2.3 More Free Time

Good time management does not mean filling up every minute with work. It means using your available hours smartly so that you complete important tasks and still have moments for fun, rest, or hobbies. That balance can boost your mood and keep you from feeling trapped in constant "busy mode."

2.4 Feeling Capable

Mastering your schedule shows you that you can solve problems and stay organized. Each time you handle multiple tasks without a meltdown, you prove to yourself you have the ability to manage your life's demands. This success feeds your sense of self-efficacy—the belief that you can handle what comes your way.

---

3. Common Time Management Problems

3.1 Procrastination

Procrastination is delaying tasks even though you know it will create stress later. For instance, waiting until the night before a test to study, or putting off a project until the last weekend. Procrastination often comes from feeling bored, intimidated by the task, or uncertain about where to start. It leads to rushed work and unnecessary worry.

3.2 Overcommitting

Saying "yes" to everything—clubs, sports, parties, extra classes—can leave you with more obligations than you can handle. You might feel pressured to keep up with your social group or fear missing out, but overloading your schedule can actually decrease your enjoyment and performance in each activity.

3.3 Lack of Goals

Sometimes you may aimlessly spend your time because you do not have clear goals. This can result in long periods of scrolling on your phone or feeling you are busy but not making real progress. Without defined targets, it is hard to set priorities or measure your success.

3.4 Poor Organization

Even if you have enough time, disorganization can waste it. Missing important deadlines because you forgot them, or spending 10 minutes searching for a lost worksheet, reflects a lack of structure. Disorganization creates chaos that eats up time you could spend more productively or enjoyably.

---

4. Planning Your Day, Week, and Month

4.1 Daily To-Do Lists

A simple starting point is making a short list of tasks for each day. Write them in a planner, a phone note, or on a piece of paper. Include things like homework assignments, chores, and personal tasks (like calling a friend or practicing an instrument). Prioritize the most urgent or important ones at the top. Checking off tasks as you complete them gives a small sense of achievement that can keep you motivated.

4.2 Weekly Overview

While daily lists help you focus on immediate tasks, a weekly plan gives you a bigger picture. You can note major assignments, club meetings, or social events on each day of the week. This helps you see busier days in advance, so you can prepare. For example, if you notice Wednesday is loaded with three activities, you might do some of your reading on Tuesday to lighten Wednesday's load.

4.3 Monthly Calendar

For exams, projects, or events that are weeks away, a monthly calendar can help you visualize upcoming deadlines. This is especially useful for big tasks that need consistent effort over time. If you know a big paper is due in three weeks, seeing it on the calendar can remind you to start early. You might mark small milestones each week to ensure you do not leave it until the last minute.

4.4 Digital vs. Paper Tools

Some people prefer paper planners because writing things down by hand helps them remember. Others enjoy digital calendars and apps that can send reminders. Try both methods and see what fits your style. The key is to use one system regularly so you do not forget tasks or mix up dates.

---

5. Prioritizing Tasks

5.1 The "Must-Do," "Should-Do," and "Could-Do" System

Not all tasks are equally important. One way to organize them is:

- **Must-Do Tasks:** These have immediate deadlines or serious consequences if not done (e.g., homework due tomorrow, a test study session, an urgent family responsibility).

- **Should-Do Tasks:** These are important but can be shifted a bit if needed (e.g., a club project due next week, tidying your room before the weekend).
- **Could-Do Tasks:** These are optional or flexible (e.g., watching a movie, browsing online for new clothes).

Handle your must-do tasks first. Then, work on the should-do tasks as time allows. Finally, if you have extra time, you can tackle the could-do tasks.

5.2 Ranking by Deadline or Impact

Another approach is to rank tasks by how soon they are due and how big an impact they have on your goals or grades. If you have a project worth a large portion of your grade but it is not due for two weeks, you might still treat it as high-priority so you can make gradual progress. Meanwhile, a small worksheet due tomorrow might be lower impact but higher urgency because of the short deadline.

5.3 Breaking Down Large Tasks

Sometimes, a large project feels overwhelming, so you push it aside. Instead, divide it into smaller parts. For a research paper, you might have steps like: choose a topic, gather sources, write an outline, draft each section, and edit. Each part has its own mini-deadline, making the process less intimidating.

5.4 Keeping Flexibility

Schedules can change. Perhaps you fall ill, or an unexpected event takes longer than planned. Include a little buffer time in your plan for each day or week if possible. This way, if something comes up, you can adjust without completely losing track of your tasks.

---

6. Avoiding Procrastination

6.1 Identify Why You Procrastinate

Common reasons include fear of failure, perfectionism, boredom, or simply not knowing how to begin. Pinpointing the cause can help you fix it. For example, if you are afraid of failing, remind yourself that trying and learning is better than not trying at all.

6.2 Use the "5-Minute Start" Trick

If a task feels too big, tell yourself you will do just five minutes of it. Often, once you start, you realize it is not so scary and continue working. The hardest part can be taking that first step.

6.3 Reward Yourself

Promise yourself a small treat—like a short break, a favorite snack, or a fun activity—after you complete a set amount of work. Knowing there is a reward can push you to start sooner. Just be sure the reward is in proportion to the task; for a small homework task, a quick 10-minute break might be enough.

6.4 Find Accountability

Share your plan with a friend or sibling, telling them, "I want to finish my science project by Wednesday." Having someone check in on you can reduce the urge to put things off. You might even do a shared study session so you can keep each other on task.

7. Scheduling Breaks and Leisure

7.1 Why Breaks Are Important

Taking breaks is not a waste of time. Brief periods of rest can help you stay sharp and prevent burnout. Just as your body needs pauses during a workout, your mind needs intervals to recharge. A short break can make you more efficient when you return to work.

7.2 The 50/10 or 25/5 Method

Some people find it effective to work for a set block of time (like 50 minutes) followed by a 10-minute break. Others prefer shorter intervals: 25 minutes of focused work, then a 5-minute break. Experiment to see what keeps you most productive without tiring you out.

7.3 Types of Breaks

- **Physical Break:** Stand up, stretch, or take a quick walk. Moving your body can refresh your mind.
- **Creative Break:** Do a small doodle, play a short tune, or write a quick message to a friend. This can keep your brain active in a different way.
- **Relaxation Break:** Close your eyes, breathe deeply, or listen to calming music. This can reduce tension and give your mind a reset.

7.4 Avoiding Over-Long Breaks

While breaks are key, be sure they do not extend indefinitely. It is easy to lose track of time scrolling through social media or chatting. Set a timer if you need to, ensuring you stick to the plan. This discipline helps you enjoy your break without falling into procrastination territory.

8. Staying Organized

8.1 Clear Workspaces

Keeping your desk or study area tidy can save time. If your notes or supplies are thrown in random places, you waste minutes finding them. A neat area also helps you focus, as there is less clutter to distract you. Take a few minutes each day to put things back where they belong.

8.2 Color-Coded Materials

Some students find color-coding notebooks or folders by subject helps them quickly grab what they need. For instance, you might keep math work in a blue folder, science in green, and language arts in red. This small system can make a big difference when you are rushing to the next class or finishing homework.

8.3 Digital Folders

If you use a laptop or tablet, organize your files into labeled folders—like "Math Homework," "Science Projects," or "Essays." Rename downloaded files with clear titles. This avoids confusion later and ensures you can find documents quickly instead of searching through random file names.

8.4 Using Timers and Reminders

Whether on your phone or a computer, set reminders for important deadlines. Some calendar apps allow you to create multiple alerts—maybe a week before a due date, two days before, and again on the morning it is due. Timers can also help you focus, as mentioned in the break method. If you have 30 minutes to finish a part of an assignment, start a timer and aim to complete it within that block.

9. Balancing School, Extracurriculars, and Personal Life

9.1 Setting Reasonable Limits

It is great to join clubs, sports, or community service. However, be honest about how many hours you actually have. If you are involved in too many activities, your academic work, health, and social life can all suffer. Choose the most meaningful clubs or teams and excel in those rather than trying to do everything.

9.2 Communication with Coaches or Advisors

If you feel overloaded, speak to the people in charge of your extracurriculars. Let them know you have a major test coming up. They might allow you some flexibility or skip a session without penalties. Most advisors prefer honest communication rather than watching you burn out.

9.3 Scheduling "Me Time"

Do not forget to schedule downtime—moments when you do something just because you enjoy it, whether that is reading a novel, playing a musical instrument for fun, or simply relaxing. This personal time helps you recharge, reducing stress and making you happier overall.

9.4 Family and Chore Coordination

If you have chores or family responsibilities, talk with your parents or guardians about your schedule. They might be willing to adjust chore times if you have a big test the next day, or you can plan your chores for a different part of the week. Open communication is key to keeping everyone on the same page.

10. Handling Unexpected Events

10.1 Flexibility Is Key

No matter how well you plan, life can throw curveballs—like sudden family obligations, illness, or last-minute group projects. Stay calm and adjust your plan instead of panicking. Move less urgent tasks to another day or see if you can finish something quicker than planned.

10.2 Building in Buffer Time

Try not to schedule every hour of your day. Leave small gaps or blocks of free time in your plan. These spare moments can absorb unforeseen delays or let you get a head start on the next day's tasks if nothing unexpected happens.

10.3 Asking for Extensions or Help

If an emergency prevents you from completing a project on time, consider respectfully asking your teacher about an extension. Explain the situation briefly and honestly. Teachers are often reasonable if you show genuine effort and communicate before the deadline passes. Similarly, do not be too proud to ask friends or family for help if you are overwhelmed.

10.4 Learning from Disruptions

Each time an unexpected event disrupts your schedule, think about what you can learn. Could you have started a task earlier? Did you fail to leave buffer time? Next time, you might adjust your approach to reduce the effect of such surprises.

11. Time Management and Mental Health

11.1 Recognizing Burnout

Burnout is a state of chronic stress and exhaustion. Signs include feeling constantly tired, losing interest in usual activities, being irritable, or having trouble focusing. If you sense these signs, it is crucial to slow down, evaluate your commitments, and restore balance.

11.2 Knowing When to Rest

Pushing yourself non-stop can lead to worse performance in the long run. Adequate sleep, healthy meals, and short mental breaks are essential for staying productive. If you notice you are consistently sleeping less than recommended (8–10 hours for most teens), consider adjusting your schedule or letting go of some obligations.

11.3 Positive Self-Talk

If you ever fall behind or miss a deadline, it is easy to flood your mind with negative thoughts like, "I am so disorganized," or "I can't do anything right." Replace these with more forgiving messages: "I had a rough week, but I'll do better next time," or "I can learn from this and make a better plan." A balanced mental approach helps you stay resilient.

11.4 Checking in with Support Systems

If stress is overwhelming, do not hesitate to talk to a school counselor, a mentor, or a trusted friend. Sometimes, just sharing your worries can lighten the load. They might also offer practical tips or reassure you that you are not alone in struggling with time pressures.

12. Real-Life Time Management Stories

12.1 Karina's Test Week Strategy

Karina had three tests in the same week. In the past, she would panic and try to cram everything the night before each test, leading to poor sleep and average grades. This time, she decided to split her study sessions over two weeks. She reviewed one subject per day, dedicating 30 to 45 minutes. She also used a weekly planner to note which topics to cover. When test week arrived, she felt prepared and slept well each night. Her scores improved, and she felt calmer overall.

12.2 Janelle's Busy Life

Janelle was on the volleyball team, worked part-time on weekends, and had a couple of advanced classes. She kept missing deadlines and arriving late to practice. Finally, she created a color-coded calendar: green for practice, blue for work shifts, and red for school tasks. She scheduled time on Tuesday and Thursday afternoons for advanced class homework. By following the plan, she reduced her lateness and had fewer late-night homework sessions. Though she sometimes had to say "no" to extra social outings, she was happier with her improved routine and better performance in sports and classes.

12.3 Mateo's Community Project

Mateo volunteered to organize a charity bake sale at school. At first, he only had a vague idea: "We'll do it next month." Soon, he realized he had to reserve a venue, gather volunteers, and promote the event. He made a timeline: 4 weeks before, secure the venue; 3 weeks before, confirm volunteer bakers; 2 weeks before, create promotional flyers; and 1 week before, collect final confirmations. This structured plan helped him avoid chaos in the final days. The bake sale went well, and Mateo felt proud of his coordination skills.

13. Practical Exercises

13.1 Time Log

For three days, record everything you do and how much time it takes. Be honest—include social media scrolling or daydreaming. Afterward, look at your log to see if any patterns jump out. Are you spending more time than you realized on non-urgent things? Could you rearrange tasks for better efficiency?

13.2 Goal Setting and Scheduling

Pick one academic goal (like improving your grade in math) and one personal goal (like practicing guitar more). Break each goal into mini-steps and decide which days you will do them. For example, "Monday, practice guitar for 20 minutes," or "Tuesday, review math notes for 15 minutes." Put these times on your calendar. Check back at the end of the week to see how it went.

13.3 Declutter Session

Take 15 minutes to tidy your study or workspace. Throw away useless papers, organize your books, and put pens in one spot. Notice if the cleaner area makes you feel more motivated or able to concentrate. Revisit this exercise once a week to maintain order.

13.4 Procrastination Buster

Pick a task you have been putting off. Set a timer for 5 minutes and promise yourself you will work on it during that short span. Often, starting is the hardest part. After 5 minutes, you might find you can continue longer or feel at least some progress made.

Chapter 15: Boundaries and Respect

1. Introduction

Boundaries and respect go hand in hand. A boundary is like an invisible line that protects your comfort, safety, and self-esteem. Respect is how you treat other people's lines as well as your own. When a person respects themselves and respects others, it builds positive relationships. If boundaries are ignored or disrespect is shown, trust breaks down, and people can get hurt—emotionally or even physically.

This chapter will walk you through what boundaries look like, why they are important, and how to communicate them in different parts of your life—at home, in friendships, in dating, and in online spaces. By the end, you should have a clearer idea of how to recognize your limits, set them confidently, and respect the limits of others. Doing this can increase your sense of safety and well-being, which can boost your self-confidence overall.

2. Understanding Boundaries

2.1 What Are Boundaries?

Boundaries are guidelines or rules you create for yourself. They tell you (and others) what you are okay with and what you are not okay with. Think of them as personal space, both emotionally and physically. For example, if you do not like people touching your hair, that is a boundary. If you want to keep certain personal details private, that is another kind of boundary.

2.2 Why They Matter

Having boundaries helps you feel safe and in control. Without them, you might feel like people can do whatever they want with your time, space, or feelings. Boundaries also teach others how to treat you. When you set a line—such as not checking your phone after 9 PM—it shows you value your mental rest. Others who care about you will respect that choice.

2.3 Types of Boundaries

1. **Physical Boundaries:** These concern your body, personal space, and privacy. Example: not wanting someone to stand too close or hug you without permission.
2. **Emotional Boundaries:** These protect your feelings and mental health. Example: letting someone know a certain topic is off-limits because it upsets you.
3. **Time Boundaries:** These deal with how you use your time. Example: choosing not to answer messages late at night so you can rest.
4. **Material Boundaries:** These cover your possessions. Example: not wanting others to borrow certain items or only lending them out under specific conditions.
5. **Digital Boundaries:** These relate to technology and online life. Example: not sharing your password or turning off notifications at certain times.

---

3. Respecting Yourself

3.1 Recognizing Your Own Worth

Before you set boundaries, you need to believe you deserve respect. If you do not value yourself, you may let others treat you poorly or invade your space. Reflect on why your well-being matters. Every person has the right to be treated with decency. Affirming your own worth is the foundation for building healthy boundaries.

3.2 Listening to Your Instincts

Your body and emotions give clues about whether a situation feels safe. Maybe your stomach tightens, or you feel anxious around a certain person. These signals can point to a boundary that needs to be set or reinforced. If you often ignore such feelings, consider slowing down and asking yourself what might be wrong. Is someone pushing you to do something you are uncomfortable with? Is someone ignoring your personal space?

3.3 Giving Yourself Permission to Say No

A big part of self-respect is understanding you are allowed to refuse requests that go against your comfort or health. Saying no does not make you rude or selfish. It simply means you are recognizing your limits. If a friend wants you to skip class, but you do not feel right about it, you can politely but firmly say no. Their reaction is not your responsibility; your well-being is.

3.4 Self-Care as a Form of Respect

Respecting yourself also means taking care of your body and mind. This can be as simple as ensuring you have enough sleep, water, and healthy food, and as personal as doing activities that help you relax. When you prioritize your own needs, you show both yourself and others that your health and happiness matter. This makes it easier to set boundaries in other areas of your life because you are used to valuing your own well-being.

---

4. Setting Boundaries with Family

4.1 Recognizing Family Dynamics

Families can be loving, but they can also be complicated. In some families, parents might expect you to share everything with them, or siblings might borrow your things without asking. In others, there may be strict rules about how you spend your time. Understanding these dynamics is the first step to figuring out where boundaries need to be placed.

4.2 Communicating Your Needs

Let your family know what you need in a calm and clear way. For instance, if you want privacy, you might say, "I need to study alone in my room for an hour. Please knock before entering." Or if you do not want a sibling taking your clothes, you might explain that it upsets you and ask them to ask permission first. If you approach these topics calmly, your family is more likely to listen.

4.3 Negotiating and Finding Middle Ground

Sometimes your family might not understand or agree with your boundary right away. They could have different views on what is normal, especially if cultural or generational differences exist. Be ready to explain why this boundary matters to you and see if you can meet halfway. Maybe they feel worried if you do not share everything, so you could set a certain time each day to talk openly—but still keep certain things private.

4.4 Handling Resistance

Your parents or siblings might resist a new boundary if it changes routines. For example, if you have always left your door open, they might feel offended when you start closing it. Stay respectful but firm. Repeat your reasons calmly. Over time, they may adjust. If they refuse to respect your boundary and it severely affects your well-being, consider talking to another family member or a counselor for guidance.

---

5. Boundaries in Friendships

5.1 Healthy vs. Unhealthy Friendships

True friends support your growth and respect your comfort zone. If a friend pressures you to do things you do not want to do—like gossiping cruelly, sharing secrets, or engaging in risky behavior—that friend might be crossing your boundaries. It is essential to know the difference between mutual respect and peer pressure or manipulation.

5.2 Saying "No" to Friends

You might feel anxious about refusing a friend because you fear losing them. But real friends value your honesty and your well-being. For instance, if your friend asks you to hang out at a time you are too busy or tired, politely say, "I can't this time, but let's plan another day." You might be surprised to find they understand. If they get angry or guilt-trip you, that could be a sign they do not truly respect you.

5.3 Handling Secret Sharing

Sometimes a friend might confide in you with sensitive information. Or they might pressure you to share your own secrets. It is okay to set boundaries around what you choose to disclose. If you do not want to talk about a personal matter, simply say, "I'm not comfortable discussing this yet." If someone is telling you secrets that make you uneasy, let them know you feel that it is too much or that you might not be able to keep it entirely to yourself if it involves danger or harm.

5.4 Online Friend Boundaries

In the digital age, friendships often include group chats, social media tags, and video calls. You can set boundaries here too. For instance, you could ask friends not to post certain photos of you without your permission. Or you can choose not to share every detail of your life on group chats. Real friends will respect your online comfort zone.

---

6. Boundaries in Romantic or Dating Relationships

6.1 Physical Boundaries

Physical boundaries in dating involve what kind of touch you are comfortable with, how quickly you want to advance, and where you draw the line. Communication is essential. If something feels too fast or just not right, let the other person know. You always have the right to say no, change your mind, or slow down.

6.2 Emotional Boundaries

Emotional closeness can be wonderful, but you might not be ready to share every secret or feeling right away. It is important to move at a pace that feels right for you. If your partner insists on knowing every detail of your life, that might be a red flag. Healthy partners respect each other's emotional space.

6.3 Respect for Each Other's Interests

Some people in relationships think they need to share all activities and interests. While shared experiences can strengthen a bond, you also need individuality. If you like reading quietly, and your partner prefers sports, it is okay to spend time apart doing different things. Pushing someone to join your hobby or giving up your interests to please them can cross personal boundaries.

6.4 Warning Signs

If a partner ignores your boundaries—like pressuring you to do something physical you are not ready for or demanding constant updates on your location—that is a sign of disrespect and possibly controlling behavior. Trust your instincts. Healthy relationships involve mutual respect, not surveillance or force. Talk to someone you trust or seek professional advice if you feel unsafe or constantly anxious about your partner's demands.

---

7. Boundaries in Online Spaces

7.1 Privacy Settings

Social media sites allow you to control who sees your posts or can message you. Take advantage of these settings. If you feel uncomfortable with strangers seeing your content, change your profile to private or limit who can contact you. Being cautious online is not about paranoia; it is about guarding your personal information and mental health.

7.2 Handling Unwanted DMs or Comments

If someone repeatedly sends you direct messages (DMs) that make you uneasy or posts rude comments on your feed, you have options. You can block them, report them, or set specific filters. You do not owe anyone your time, especially if they disrespect you. Recognize that it is your right to maintain a digital boundary.

7.3 Sharing Personal Information

Decide in advance what personal details you will never share online—like your home address, phone number, or private photos. Let your close friends know you do not want them tagging you with location details or posting pictures that reveal personal info. This is crucial for safety as well as preserving your mental space.

7.4 Digital Detoxes or Time-Off Boundaries

Sometimes, you might choose to step away from social media or turn off your phone for certain hours to reduce stress. This is a boundary you set for yourself. Tell friends or followers that you will not be available after a certain time or for a particular day. This helps you maintain a healthy balance with technology.

---

8. Respecting Others' Boundaries

8.1 Recognizing and Valuing Their Limits

Respect goes both ways. If a friend says, "I don't like hugging," do not force them. If a sibling says they need quiet time, do your best to honor that. Letting others have their personal space fosters mutual trust. This reciprocity—both sides respecting each other—builds stronger, healthier connections.

8.2 Asking for Consent

Consent is not just about physical contact; it applies to many actions. For example, before sharing a group photo that includes others, ask if they are okay with it being posted. Or before borrowing an item, request permission. These small acts of respect show you value people's comfort and property.

8.3 Listening Without Judgment

If someone sets a boundary, you might not fully understand it. But you can still accept it. For instance, if a friend says they do not want to discuss a certain topic, avoid pushing them. They have their reasons. By respecting that limit, you show empathy and consideration.

8.4 Apologizing if You Cross a Line

Mistakes happen. You might share a private story you thought was harmless, only to realize your friend wanted to keep it secret. In such cases, apologize sincerely. Explain that you did not intend harm, promise not to do it again, and respect any new boundary they set to prevent a similar incident in the future.

---

9. Communicating Boundaries Clearly

9.1 Use Simple, Direct Language

When stating a boundary, clarity is key. Phrases like, "I'd like you to knock before coming in," or "I don't feel comfortable talking about that subject," are straightforward. Avoid vague hints. The more clear you are, the less room there is for confusion.

9.2 Stay Firm, but Polite

You can be respectful and firm at the same time. For example, "I understand you want to hang out, but I've already made plans to study tonight. Let's find another day," has a calm tone. You do not need to over-explain or apologize repeatedly for having personal limits.

9.3 Offer Alternatives (Sometimes)

If saying no feels harsh, you can suggest another option that fits your comfort zone. For instance, "I'm not okay giving you my phone password, but I can show you the text if you want to read it," or "I can't lend you my new sweater, but you can borrow another one if you like."

9.4 Practice in Low-Stress Situations

If you struggle with boundary setting, practice in smaller scenarios first. For example, politely but firmly refuse a treat you do not want, or ask a friend to please not photograph you at a certain moment. Getting comfortable with minor boundaries builds your confidence for bigger, more sensitive ones.

---

10. Overcoming Guilt and Fear

10.1 Understanding Emotional Barriers

Many people avoid setting boundaries because they feel guilty. They worry about hurting feelings or appearing selfish. Others feel fear—fear of conflict, rejection, or losing relationships. Recognize these emotions as natural but not necessarily accurate. Protecting your well-being is not selfish, and kind people will usually understand you need personal space.

10.2 Reframing "Selfishness"

Acting in your own best interest is not always selfish. Selfishness typically means ignoring or harming others for your own gain. Setting healthy boundaries is about taking care of yourself without hurting others. In fact, clear boundaries often prevent resentment from building up, which can actually make relationships healthier.

10.3 Tolerating Other People's Reactions

Sometimes, people might react poorly to your boundaries because they are used to having certain freedoms with you. They might complain or sulk. That does not automatically mean you have done something wrong. Stand by your decision unless you realize you truly want to adjust it. Over time, friends or family who respect you will adapt.

10.4 Seeking Support

If you are struggling with guilt or fear, talk to someone you trust—a counselor, mentor, or close friend. They can offer perspective and remind you why your boundaries matter. In some cases, hearing encouragement from an outside source can reinforce your resolve and help you overcome emotional roadblocks.

---

11. When Boundaries Are Disrespected Repeatedly

11.1 Recognizing Patterns

If a person continually ignores your requests or invades your space, take notice. One slip can be a mistake, but repeated disrespect might indicate a deeper problem. This pattern might occur in family relationships, friendships, or romantic connections. Pay attention to how often it happens and whether they apologize or change their behavior afterward.

11.2 Deciding Next Steps

Ask yourself how serious the boundary violations are. If someone occasionally forgets to knock and then apologizes, you might just need to remind them. But if a friend or partner regularly pushes you into uncomfortable situations or humiliates you, you might need to limit contact or end the relationship. Only you can gauge how damaging it is to your sense of safety and self-worth.

11.3 Seeking Mediation

For ongoing boundary conflicts—like a sibling borrowing your things without permission—a neutral third party can help mediate. This could be a parent, teacher, or counselor who listens to both sides and suggests a fair solution. Having a calm environment and a guiding figure can reduce tension and clarify misunderstandings.

11.4 Walking Away

In the worst cases, if someone refuses to respect your boundaries and their actions harm you, walking away may be necessary. This can be emotionally tough but is sometimes the healthiest choice. Whether it is a friend who always mocks your personal values or a partner who disrespects your physical limits, your well-being should remain the priority.

---

12. Real-Life Scenarios

12.1 Ava's Study Time Boundary

Ava's parents often walked into her room to check on her while she was studying, making it hard to concentrate. She decided to set a boundary by telling them, "Could you please knock before coming in? I lose focus when I'm interrupted." At first, they seemed surprised, but they gradually respected her request. Ava found her study sessions became more productive, and her parents appreciated her calmer mood.

12.2 Marco and Friends' Group Chat

Marco was in a group chat that never seemed to stop buzzing. His phone went off late at night with memes and random jokes. He found himself tired at school the next day because he kept checking messages. He finally set a boundary by turning off notifications after 9 PM and telling his friends, "I'm muting the group at night, but I'll catch up in the morning." Though a few friends teased him for it, they ultimately left him alone at night. Marco's sleep and mental well-being improved.

12.3 Tia's Over-Borrowing Cousin

Tia's cousin always borrowed her clothes without asking and even left them in poor condition. Tia felt uncomfortable but did not want to seem mean. She finally approached her cousin and said, "I'd prefer that you ask before borrowing anything. Also, if you return something damaged, please replace it or fix it." Her cousin initially got defensive but later realized Tia had a fair point. They worked out a system to share clothes with proper care and permission.

12.4 Nina's Relationship Concern

Nina started dating someone who wanted to check her phone regularly. She felt uneasy but did not want to upset her partner. Over time, she realized this was a boundary being crossed. She said, "I'm not comfortable with you going through my messages. I need privacy." When her partner insisted that "trust means sharing everything," Nina stood firm and repeated her stance. Eventually, she saw this demand as a sign of controlling behavior and chose to end the relationship to protect her sense of independence.

---

13. Practical Exercises

13.1 Boundary Identification List

Write down different areas of your life—school, home, friendships, romantic connections, online. Under each category, note any situation that makes you uncomfortable or stressed. Then describe the ideal boundary for each. For example, "School: I don't like lending notes without guarantee of return. Boundary: Must get notes back in one week." Seeing this list clarifies where you need to speak up.

13.2 Practice Scripts

For each boundary, create a short phrase to communicate it. Examples might be:

- "I'm studying right now; can we talk after I'm done?"
- "Please don't post photos of me without asking."
- "I need some alone time tonight."

Practice saying these out loud, even if it feels awkward. This makes it easier to voice them in real situations because you have prepared the words in advance.

13.3 Observe and Respect Day

Choose one day to focus on respecting others' boundaries. Notice when someone mentions not wanting to talk about something or needing space. Respond positively, like, "Sure, no problem." Reflect at day's end on how it felt to consciously honor those limits. This can increase your empathy for others' boundaries and make you more attuned to your own.

13.4 Imagining the Worst-Case

Sometimes fear holds you back from stating boundaries. Ask yourself, "What is the worst thing that could happen if I say no?" Often, you realize the worst-case scenario—like a brief argument or someone being annoyed—is not that terrible. Putting it in perspective can reduce anxiety around boundary setting.

Chapter 16: Habits for Self-Care

1. Introduction

Self-care is about taking steps to maintain or improve your health, mood, and overall well-being. It includes daily habits, mindful practices, and small choices that keep you balanced. For teen girls, self-care can be especially important because of the changes and challenges you face—academic pressure, social expectations, and personal development.

Many people assume self-care is just about pampering yourself or indulging in luxuries. In reality, real self-care is more than occasional treats. It is about committing to regular, healthy routines that support your physical, mental, and emotional stability. This chapter explores different forms of self-care, from physical exercises to mental breaks and creativity. By the end, you should have a range of ideas to incorporate into your daily life, helping you feel stronger, calmer, and more confident.

2. What Is Self-Care?

2.1 Basic Definition

Self-care means actions you take to protect and nurture yourself—body and mind. It goes beyond mere relaxation. True self-care helps you recover from stress, prevent burnout, and handle day-to-day challenges more effectively. It can be as simple as drinking enough water or as structured as setting aside time each week for a hobby.

2.2 Why It's Not Selfish

Some people think focusing on personal well-being is selfish. But if you do not care for yourself, you might burn out and become less able to help others. Think of it like putting on your oxygen mask first on an airplane. You cannot assist anyone else if you are gasping for air. When you are well-rested and mentally healthy, you are better equipped to show up for friends and family.

2.3 The Role of Habits

Self-care becomes most effective when it is built into your daily routine. Habits are actions you do automatically, like brushing your teeth. If you rely on willpower alone, you might skip self-care on busy or stressful days. Turning self-care into a regular habit ensures it remains consistent, regardless of external pressures.

---

3. Physical Self-Care Habits

3.1 Prioritizing Sleep

Getting enough sleep—generally 8 to 10 hours for teens—is fundamental. During sleep, your body repairs itself, and your mind processes the day's events. Chronic lack of sleep can lead to low energy, mood swings, and trouble concentrating. Small steps, like avoiding screens before bed and setting a consistent bedtime, can greatly improve sleep quality.

3.2 Balanced Nutrition

What you eat directly affects your energy levels and mood. A balanced diet includes a mix of proteins, carbohydrates, healthy fats, fruits, and vegetables. This does not mean you must cut out all treats. Aim for moderation. If you find you are skipping meals or always snacking on junk food, try planning simple, balanced meals. Even small changes, like adding an extra serving of fruit or vegetables daily, can make a difference.

3.3 Regular Movement

You do not have to be a star athlete to benefit from physical activity. Walking, dancing, cycling, or even doing short home workouts can help your body and mind. Exercise releases endorphins, chemicals that improve your mood. Pick activities that you enjoy rather than forcing yourself to do something boring or extreme. Consistency is the key—try to move at least a few days a week.

3.4 Hydration and Personal Hygiene

Drinking enough water helps maintain energy levels and clear thinking. Personal hygiene, like taking regular showers, brushing your teeth, and washing your face, is also part of caring for your body. Good hygiene can help prevent health issues and even lift your mood, as feeling clean and fresh often leads to a sense of well-being.

---

4. Mental and Emotional Self-Care

4.1 Journaling Your Thoughts

Writing down your worries or reflections in a journal can help you process emotions. You do not need to be a great writer; just be honest. Maybe you jot down a few lines about your day, things you are grateful for, or goals for tomorrow. Journaling can relieve stress because it gets thoughts out of your head and onto paper, making them feel more manageable.

4.2 Mindfulness and Breathing Exercises

Mindfulness involves paying attention to the present moment without judgment. A simple practice is closing your eyes and focusing on your breathing. If thoughts pop up, acknowledge them, but gently bring your focus back to your breath. Even doing this for a couple of minutes can calm racing thoughts. Over time, mindfulness can help you cope better with stress and anxiety.

4.3 Limiting Negative Input

Sometimes, emotional strain comes from constant exposure to negative influences—like toxic social media accounts or gossip-heavy conversations. Part of self-care is noticing when such negativity affects your mood. You might choose to unfollow certain accounts, limit time with pessimistic people, or cut back on news consumption that leaves you feeling helpless. This boundary protects your mental space.

4.4 Seeking Support or Therapy

If stress or low mood is overwhelming, consider talking to a counselor or therapist. This is not a sign of weakness—it is a proactive step toward well-being. Professionals can offer tools to handle anxiety, depression, or other challenges. Even if you feel generally okay, occasional therapy sessions can provide a healthy outlet to discuss concerns without fear of judgment.

---

5. Social Self-Care

5.1 Building a Support Network

Humans are social creatures. Having people you can turn to—friends, family members, or mentors—greatly aids emotional resilience. A support network is a group of individuals who respect your boundaries and celebrate your growth. Cultivate this network by staying in touch with caring friends, reaching out to relatives you trust, or joining groups around your interests.

5.2 Setting Social Boundaries

While connection is vital, too much social time or the wrong kind of socializing can wear you down. It is okay to say no to a hangout if you need alone time. Or, if certain gatherings always leave you feeling upset, think about limiting your involvement or going with a supportive friend. Balancing social interaction with personal space helps you keep a healthy social life.

5.3 Quality Over Quantity

It is tempting to think having many friends or a large online following means a better social life. However, genuine connections often matter more than numbers. A few close friends who truly understand you can offer deeper support than a wide circle of acquaintances. Focus on strengthening relationships that are built on trust, respect, and shared values.

5.4 Safe Online Communities

If you enjoy connecting online, look for supportive communities or forums. Some places focus on mental health awareness, hobbies, or positive reinforcement. Avoid spaces full of drama or bullying. Online friendships can be real and meaningful, but treat them like any relationship—set boundaries, choose carefully, and avoid oversharing personal information too quickly.

---

6. Relaxation Techniques

6.1 Guided Imagery

This practice involves closing your eyes and imagining a calming scene. It could be a peaceful beach, a forest trail, or a cozy room. Picture the details—colors, sounds, textures, scents. Let yourself mentally "stay" in this scene for a few minutes, breathing slowly. This can lower stress and bring a sense of calm, especially before bed or during breaks.

6.2 Progressive Muscle Relaxation

In this exercise, you tense a muscle group for a few seconds and then release it. Start with your toes, move up to your calves, thighs, stomach, arms, and face. Notice the difference between tension and relaxation in each area. This method can relieve physical tension stored up from stress and is easy to do at home.

6.3 Soothing Activities

Activities like coloring, knitting, or creating collages can have a calming effect. The repetitive motions or focus on detail help shift your mind away from worries. If you enjoy music, try playing an instrument or listening to relaxing tunes. The goal is to find something that occupies your hands or mind in a mellow way, providing a mental break from daily pressures.

6.4 Nature Time

Spending time outdoors is another form of relaxation. You could sit on a park bench, go for a walk, or even just observe the sky. Studies suggest being around greenery or natural elements can reduce stress hormones and improve mood. If you cannot get to a large park, you can try tending to houseplants or simply enjoying the sunlight on your porch.

---

7. Creative Outlets

7.1 Expressing Emotions Through Art

Drawing, painting, writing, or crafting can help you deal with feelings in a constructive way. You do not need professional skills to benefit. The act of creating something—be it a poem or a doodle—allows you to release tension or explore thoughts you cannot put into simple words.

7.2 Music and Dance

Whether you sing, play an instrument, or just move to your favorite tunes, music-related activities can uplift your spirit. Dancing can be both physical exercise and emotional expression. You might find that belting out a song or doing a short dance routine shifts your mood almost immediately.

7.3 Cooking and Baking

For some, cooking or baking becomes a delightful ritual. The process of measuring, mixing, and tasting can feel soothing. Plus, the result is often something you can enjoy with friends or family. Just be mindful if you have a busy schedule—avoid overly complex recipes that add stress instead of reducing it.

7.4 Shared Creative Sessions

Gathering with friends for a craft night or music jam can combine social interaction with creativity, doubling the self-care benefits. Even virtual sessions work if you have online friends who want to collaborate on art projects or share writing ideas. This group dynamic can spark inspiration and deepen friendships.

---

8. Structuring Self-Care into Your Routine

8.1 Small Daily Habits

Instead of making self-care a big event only on weekends, try brief daily habits. Examples could include:

- Writing a sentence of gratitude each morning.
- Doing a 5-minute stretch or breathing exercise.
- Having a screen-free hour before bedtime.
- Drinking a glass of water upon waking up.

These small steps add up over time, creating a steady foundation for well-being.

8.2 Weekly "Reset" Day

Pick one day a week, maybe Sunday, to check in with yourself. You could plan your week's schedule, tidy your room, or do a longer self-care activity like a home spa or extended reading session. This "reset" helps you start the new week with a clear mind and organized environment.

8.3 Personal Goals for Improvement

If there is a particular area you want to improve—like stress management or fitness—include it in your routine. For instance, plan three short workouts a week or schedule a 10-minute mindfulness session each day.

Track your progress to see how these habits impact your mood and stress levels.

8.4 Adapting to Changes

Life circumstances change—school schedules, family obligations, or personal interests. Your self-care routine might need adjustments. Stay flexible. If you realize you are too busy to do a long activity, shorten it rather than dropping it altogether. The goal is consistency, not perfection.

---

9. Overcoming Obstacles to Self-Care

9.1 Feeling Too Busy

You might say, "I have zero time for self-care." However, often there are pockets of time that go unused—like waiting for the bus or scrolling through social media aimlessly. Consider replacing some of that time with quick self-care tasks: deep breathing, jotting down thoughts, or reading a positive article.

9.2 Guilt About Putting Yourself First

As mentioned, self-care is not selfish. Yet guilt can creep in, especially if family or friends demand your attention. Remember that by tending to your own needs, you ultimately show up as a calmer, more helpful person for them. It is about balance—helping others does not mean neglecting yourself.

9.3 Social Pressure

Sometimes, peers tease or misunderstand your self-care decisions. For example, if you choose not to stay up late gaming because you value sleep, they might call you boring. Stick to your boundaries and remind yourself why you made the choice. Real friends should support your well-being rather than mock it.

9.4 Lack of Motivation

Starting a new habit can feel hard, especially when you are tired or discouraged. Break it down into very small steps. If you cannot do a 30-minute workout, do 5 minutes. If writing a journal feels overwhelming, just write a single line. Doing something is better than doing nothing. Over time, these small acts can build motivation.

---

10. Self-Care and Self-Confidence

10.1 Seeing Progress

When you consistently practice self-care, you might notice you have more energy, clearer skin, or improved mood. These positive changes reinforce the idea that your efforts matter. Recognizing your ability to influence your well-being can boost self-confidence.

10.2 Increased Emotional Stability

Dealing with stress or setbacks becomes easier if you have built a strong foundation of self-care. You may recover faster from disappointments because your mind and body are in a healthier state. This stability helps you believe in your resilience.

10.3 Self-Worth Validation

When you dedicate time to caring for yourself, you send yourself a message that you are important and deserve attention. Over time, this can undo negative beliefs like "I'm not worthy" or "I should always put others first." Self-care becomes an act of self-respect, showing you that you matter.

10.4 Leading by Example

When peers or younger siblings see you maintaining balanced habits—like making time to rest, exercising, or managing your stress calmly—they might follow suit. Becoming a role model in self-care can further affirm your confidence. You realize your actions positively affect others, strengthening your sense of purpose and self-esteem.

---

11. Signs You Need More Self-Care

11.1 Persistent Exhaustion

If you frequently wake up feeling drained or rely on caffeine just to get through the day, it may indicate you need better rest and calmer evenings. Evaluate your sleep schedule and see if late-night phone use or inconsistent bedtime is the culprit.

11.2 Constant Irritability

Feeling easily annoyed by small things can signal emotional overload. You might lack an outlet for stress or be taking on too many responsibilities. A bit more "me time" or a break in your schedule could help you reset.

11.3 Loss of Interest

If you stop enjoying hobbies or activities you once loved, it could be a warning sign of burnout or low mood. Injecting more self-care—like creative outlets or social breaks—might bring back your enthusiasm. If the feeling persists, consider talking to a counselor.

11.4 Physical Issues

Headaches, frequent colds, or other minor health problems can sometimes stem from stress or poor routine. While you should rule out medical causes, also assess whether you are skipping meals, sleeping poorly, or ignoring the need for mental breaks.

12. Real-Life Self-Care Examples

12.1 Ava's Quick Morning Routine

Ava used to hit the snooze button multiple times, then rush to school feeling groggy. She decided to wake up just 15 minutes earlier to stretch, drink a glass of water, and review a simple list of daily goals. Although it was only a quarter-hour difference, she noticed she felt less frantic and more centered. This small change set a calm tone for her entire day.

12.2 Jacob's Art Breaks

Jacob had a busy schedule with sports and advanced classes. He rarely had a chance to recharge. He started bringing a small sketchpad to school. During lunch or study hall, he would draw for 5 minutes. This brief creative activity helped him clear his mind before returning to work. Over time, he found that his concentration improved, and he looked forward to these mini art breaks as a stress reliever.

12.3 Mia's Tech-Free Evenings

Mia realized she was staying up too late, scrolling on social media. She then struggled to wake up on time. She set a rule to stop using her phone after 9 PM and plugged it in away from her bed. The first week was hard, as she missed the constant feed of updates. But she soon noticed she slept better and felt sharper in the morning. She also discovered she had time for reading, which she found surprisingly peaceful.

12.4 Eric's Weekly "Walk and Talk"

Eric noticed he was increasingly stressed about school drama and felt isolated. He decided to invite a close friend for a weekly walk around the neighborhood. They chatted about their week, vented frustrations, and encouraged each other. This routine offered both physical exercise and emotional support. Eric's mood lifted, and his friend felt the same benefits.

13. Practical Exercises

13.1 Five-Minute Mindful Break

Set a timer for five minutes. Close your eyes, breathe naturally, and focus on how your breath feels. If thoughts or worries arise, acknowledge them briefly but guide your attention back to your breathing. Try this once or twice a day for a week. Notice any change in your stress level or focus.

13.2 Gratitude Notes

Each evening, write down at least three small things you are grateful for. They could be as simple as enjoying a tasty snack or getting a nice text from a friend. Reflecting on positives can shift your mindset and reduce the tendency to dwell on negatives.

13.3 Self-Care Calendar

Design a small calendar (digital or paper) for a month. Assign a different self-care task to each day—like stretching, reading a poem, or trying a new recipe. Check off each day's activity once completed. This adds variety to your routine and keeps self-care interesting.

13.4 Feel-Good Folder

Create a digital or physical folder where you store positive messages, compliments, or memories—such as screenshots of kind texts, photos of happy moments, or notes from friends. On days you feel low, revisit this folder. It can be a quick emotional boost and reminder that you are valued.

Chapter 17: Finding Your Interests

1. Introduction

Many people say, "Follow your passions," but as a teen girl, you might still be unsure what truly excites or motivates you. Society and social media can push certain trends, leaving you feeling uncertain if your interests are genuine or just influenced by friends or the internet. This confusion is normal. In fact, these teenage years are a prime time to explore different activities, subjects, and possible career paths.

Discovering what you like is not just about choosing a future job. It is also about understanding yourself better. When you spend time on activities that spark your curiosity, you grow more confident in your abilities. You learn how to solve problems, handle challenges, and maybe even find new friends who share similar passions. This chapter will explore why your interests matter, how to find them, and ways to keep them alive even when obstacles pop up.

The goal is to help you see that exploring your interests is a process, not a test you can fail. Every new class, club, or hobby you try can teach you something—either by showing you what you like or by clarifying what you do not enjoy. By the end, you will have a clearer sense of how to identify areas that genuinely speak to you, along with strategies for staying engaged and enthusiastic about them.

2. Why Interests Matter

2.1 Boosting Confidence

One of the strongest reasons to find your interests is the boost in self-confidence that comes from doing something you enjoy or value. When you work on a subject or hobby that truly resonates with you, you often put forth more effort and see better results. Positive feedback, personal pride, and a feeling of achievement can increase your belief in yourself. Over time, this belief extends to other parts of your life, helping you handle challenges with a more secure mindset.

2.2 Forming Friendships

Shared interests often bring people together. Whether it is a music club, a sports team, or an art class, when you find an activity you care about, you are likely to meet others who feel the same way. These shared experiences can lead to strong friendships because you have a common ground. You might collaborate on projects, learn from each other, or simply bond over the joy you get from the activity. This social connection can further strengthen your confidence and sense of belonging.

2.3 Reducing Stress

Life can feel chaotic with school, family duties, and social matters. Having an interest that helps you unwind can provide a mental break. Engaging in a fun or meaningful activity can lower stress levels, give your mind a chance to rest, and remind you that there is more to life than just obligations. Even if you only have a few free hours each week, dedicating that time to an enjoyable pastime can refresh your outlook and mood.

2.4 Direction and Motivation

Finding your interests can also guide your decisions for the future. For instance, if you love writing, you might explore related fields like journalism or creative writing down the road. If you are drawn to science experiments, that interest might lead you to pursue more advanced classes or research opportunities. Having a direction, even if it changes later, can give you an extra push to keep learning and growing.

3. Exploring Different Activities

3.1 Sampling Clubs and Events

Your school likely offers a variety of clubs—language clubs, drama, debate, robotics, art, cooking, and so on. You do not have to stick with one forever. Trying out a few clubs just to see what they are about can open your eyes to new hobbies or fields of study. If your school hosts activity fairs or has sign-up booths, take a quick look at each booth that grabs your attention. You might end up joining a club you never knew existed.

If clubs are not your style, look for events in your community—a weekend workshop on coding, a library talk on local history, or a free art exhibit. Attending these events, even if you go alone at first, can expose you to fresh ideas. You might find that seeing people who are passionate about something sparks your own curiosity.

3.2 Online Resources and Tutorials

The internet provides endless tutorials and videos on just about every topic. If you are curious about photography, you can watch basic lessons on camera settings and composition. If cooking draws you in, you can find step-by-step recipes with videos that guide you. Do a quick search for a skill or topic you think might be interesting. Spend an afternoon exploring beginner tips. If it clicks with you, great; if not, you have only spent a short time.

3.3 Volunteering Opportunities

Volunteering is another way to find your interests. By helping out at an animal shelter, you might discover a passion for animal welfare or veterinary science. Volunteering at a community garden might reveal an interest in the environment or agriculture. These experiences also let you see firsthand the impact of your efforts, which can be incredibly rewarding and might uncover a new field you feel strongly about.

3.4 Talking to People with Different Hobbies

Sometimes the best way to learn about a field is to talk to someone already involved. If you know a friend, neighbor, or relative who has an interesting job or hobby, ask them about it. How did they get started? What do they enjoy most? What challenges do they face? Hearing personal stories can inspire you to try something you might never have considered.

---

4. Overcoming the Fear of Failure

4.1 Accepting Mistakes as Part of Learning

When exploring interests, many teens worry about not being "good enough" right away. But learning a new skill almost always involves messing up. Pianists play wrong notes. Writers produce weak drafts. Athletes stumble in practice. Mistakes are part of the process. Instead of seeing them as proof you lack talent, view them as steps toward improvement.

4.2 Keeping a Beginner's Mind

When you start something new, you are not expected to be an expert. Approaching the activity with a "beginner's mind" means you accept that you have a lot to learn, and that is okay. This mindset reduces pressure and allows you to enjoy the learning experience. Over time, consistent practice will likely produce better results, but do not rush that stage. Embrace the fun of discovering something for the first time.

4.3 Shifting from Results to Enjoyment

If you focus too much on end results—like a perfect painting or a flawless performance—you might forget to enjoy the actual process. Try to measure your satisfaction by how engaged you feel or how much you learn, rather than by how you compare to others. People who stick with their interests usually do so because they find pleasure in the day-to-day challenge and not just the final outcome.

4.4 Encouraging Self-Talk

When doubt creeps in, remind yourself you have the right to explore. There is no universal rule saying you have to be perfect immediately. Speak kindly in your own head: "I'm new at this, and that's okay," or "Everyone starts somewhere." Positive self-talk can reduce the fear that sometimes blocks you from discovering what you love.

---

5. Setting Mini-Goals for Growth

5.1 Why Mini-Goals Help

Breaking your learning path into smaller targets can keep you motivated. Instead of saying, "I want to be a great coder," you might say, "By the end of this month, I'll learn how to create a simple webpage." Mini-goals let you see progress more often, which boosts confidence. Achieving a small milestone can feel just as satisfying and spurs you to keep going.

5.2 Examples of Mini-Goals

- **Art:** Complete a small sketch or painting each week.
- **Music:** Learn to play one short song on an instrument by the end of two weeks.
- **Language Learning:** Memorize 10 new words or phrases a week.
- **Sports:** Practice a specific technique (like dribbling in basketball or serving in tennis) for 20 minutes a day, five days a week.

5.3 Tracking Progress

Use a notebook, calendar, or an app to mark when you achieve each mini-goal. This record serves as proof of how far you have come and can encourage you to keep pushing. If you miss a mini-goal or fall behind, do not see it as a failure. Adjust your plan, maybe make smaller goals, or give yourself a bit more time. The main idea is to keep momentum.

5.4 Rewarding Yourself

Offering yourself small rewards can make the process more fun. This could be as simple as allowing 30 minutes of extra reading time, a relaxing bath, or a special snack you enjoy once you finish a week of consistent practice. Rewards, combined with the inherent joy of progress, can motivate you to stick with your interest long enough to see if it is truly right for you.

---

6. Trying Clubs, Teams, and Workshops

6.1 Club Advantages

Joining a club in school or within the community can provide structure around your interest. Regular meetings, group projects, or competitions can help you dive deeper than you might on your own. You also get the support of peers who are learning alongside you, which can make the experience more enjoyable and less intimidating.

6.2 Sports Teams

If your interest leans toward physical activity, trying a sports team can teach discipline, teamwork, and resilience. Even if you do not end up loving that particular sport, you might discover you enjoy being active and later switch to a different sport or fitness routine. Keep in mind that you do not have to be the star player; participating and improving at your own pace can be valuable as well.

6.3 Workshops or Short Courses

Some schools, community centers, or local colleges offer short workshops. These can range from cooking classes to robotics boot camps. A short class can be a low-commitment way to see if you really like something. If you find it captivating, you can sign up for more advanced courses or join related activities.

6.4 Overcoming Initial Nerves

The idea of walking into a room full of strangers who already seem to know what they are doing can feel scary. Remind yourself that many clubs are designed to welcome newcomers. You can also bring a friend if that helps. The first few sessions might feel awkward, but usually, people appreciate fresh faces and new perspectives.

---

7. Tools for Self-Discovery

7.1 Personality Quizzes and Aptitude Tests

While they are not perfect, personality quizzes and aptitude tests can offer hints about areas you might find interesting or excel in. Some tests measure if you lean toward creative, analytical, or practical tasks. They might also suggest career paths or hobbies that fit your general traits. Use these results as inspiration, not absolute rules.

7.2 Journaling and Reflection

Keeping a journal where you note what activities you enjoyed each day (or each week) can highlight patterns. Maybe you notice you consistently feel happy after helping a friend with math or after reading an article about wildlife conservation. Over time, these observations can point to deeper interests you did not realize were there.

7.3 Talking to Counselors or Mentors

School counselors can sometimes provide insight into clubs, internships, or volunteer roles that match your skills. Mentors—like a teacher you trust or a family friend—may share their own experiences and guide you toward resources. They might even connect you with professionals in a field you want to learn more about.

7.4 Vision Boards or Simple Lists

Creating a vision board (online or on paper) with pictures and words that resonate with you can serve as motivation. Alternatively, writing a list of "Topics/Skills That Spark My Interest" can provide clarity. Revisit this board or list occasionally, adding or removing items as you learn more about yourself.

---

8. Real-Life Stories of Teens Finding Their Passions

8.1 Sara's Science Discovery

Sara joined the science club mostly because her best friend did. At first, she felt a bit out of place during experiments. But when she got assigned to a project about plant growth under different lights, something clicked. She found herself staying after school to observe the plants and record data meticulously. By the end of the semester, she realized she actually loved biology. She then signed up for an advanced biology class and started reading science magazines. Her curiosity in science led her to volunteer at a local nature reserve, and now she envisions studying environmental science in college.

8.2 Kevin's Surprise Love for Poetry

Kevin had always been more into sports, but he ended up in a creative writing elective because other classes were full. To his surprise, writing short poems gave him a rush of excitement. He enjoyed playing with words and developing emotional depth. Though initially shy about sharing, he read one poem at a school event. The positive response boosted his confidence, and he realized that writing allowed him to express thoughts he could not put into regular conversation. He continued with sports but balanced that with writing practice, finding joy in both physical and creative outlets.

8.3 Rina's Art Transition

Rina tried a painting class over the summer because she wanted to fill her vacation. She liked it but found the step-by-step instructions dull. Later, she discovered street art and graffiti culture through a documentary and felt more attracted to that style. She began creating digital designs, then printed them as stickers. Her classmates admired her unique style. While she still respects traditional painting, her true passion blossomed in digital street art. This path taught her that even within the same field—like art—there can be many branches to explore.

8.4 Omar's Gaming Turned Programming

Omar loved playing video games. He spent hours analyzing game mechanics and storylines. At first, he felt guilty about the time spent gaming. Then, a friend told him about free online coding lessons to build simple games. Omar tried it and realized he liked the programming side of games even more than just playing. He started making small puzzle games, learning more each time. This new skill boosted his self-confidence because he saw he could transform a casual interest into something creative and maybe even career-related.

---

9. Practical Tips for Keeping Interests Alive

9.1 Allocate Time Each Week

Schedule a slot in your calendar for your chosen activity—maybe an hour or two each week where you focus on your interest without distractions. Treat it like an important appointment with yourself. Overloading your schedule can lead to neglecting your interest, so plan realistically.

9.2 Find a Supportive Community

Whether online or offline, look for groups that share your passion. This could be a subreddit about writing, a local photography club, or a sports training group. Being around others who understand your excitement can keep you motivated, especially when you feel discouraged or stuck.

9.3 Keep Learning

Even if you start becoming good at something, there is always more to learn. Keep challenging yourself with harder pieces of music, new painting styles, or advanced coding concepts. Constant learning keeps your interest from going stale and makes you see that there is always more to discover.

9.4 Avoid Overcommitment

While enthusiasm is great, be careful not to bite off more than you can chew. If you join five clubs at once, you might burn out and lose your initial joy. Start with one or two activities, see how they fit into your life, and then add more if you genuinely have the time and energy.

---

10. Balancing Responsibilities and Interests

10.1 Time Management Strategies

Your daily life likely includes school, family tasks, and maybe part-time work or extracurriculars. To fit in your interest, use basic time management. Create a small to-do list or plan your day, prioritizing mandatory tasks first. Then, place your hobby or passion in an open slot. Even 30 minutes a day can keep your interest going.

10.2 Avoiding Guilt

You might feel guilty spending time on a hobby instead of studying. The truth is, having a healthy outlet can actually improve your overall performance. Your brain needs breaks to function well. As long as you do not neglect important duties, investing time in something you care about can help you feel balanced and less stressed.

10.3 Handling Pressure from Others

Sometimes parents or friends may question why you spend time on certain hobbies. If they express concern that it is a waste of time, calmly explain why it matters to you. Show how you are still keeping up with school or other obligations. Communicating your perspective can help them see your interest as a positive element rather than a distraction.

10.4 Knowing When to Adjust

Interests can evolve. If you find that a certain activity is causing more stress than joy, step back and reassess. Maybe you loved debate club at first, but now it feels overwhelming. It is okay to pause or switch gears. The aim is to learn and grow, not to lock yourself into something that no longer serves you.

Chapter 18: Dealing with Changes

1. Introduction

Life changes constantly. As a teen girl, you might be facing new environments, shifting friendships, or evolving family dynamics. You could be moving to a different school, noticing changes in your physical appearance, or experiencing the end of certain childhood routines. All of these changes can bring both excitement and anxiety.

Learning to handle change in a positive way can build your resilience and self-confidence. When you adapt to new situations, you prove to yourself that you are capable and strong. This chapter dives into common changes teens go through, why they can be difficult, and how to approach them with balance. By the end, you will have strategies for handling change that can lower your stress and help you find opportunities in the midst of uncertainty.

2. Recognizing Types of Changes

2.1 Physical Changes

During adolescence, your body goes through many shifts—growth spurts, hormonal changes, and other developments that might leave you feeling awkward or self-conscious. Learning to care for your changing body, maintaining hygiene, and seeking reliable information about physical health can lessen feelings of embarrassment or confusion.

2.2 Emotional Changes

Your emotional world can also fluctuate. Mood swings, stronger feelings of anger or sadness, and deeper empathy for others are common experiences. Developing emotional awareness—knowing when you are upset, why you feel that way, and how to cope—helps prevent emotional outbursts and fosters healthier relationships.

2.3 Social Changes

Friend groups can change. You might drift apart from friends you knew in elementary school or meet new people in clubs. Family roles can also shift—maybe you have younger siblings who now look up to you, or older relatives who expect more maturity from you. These social changes can lead to a sense of confusion about where you fit in, but they can also open the door to new friendships and stronger bonds.

2.4 Academic or Career-Related Changes

Moving from one grade level to another often brings tougher classes and higher expectations. You might also start considering college or career paths, which adds pressure to your choices of clubs, extracurriculars, or the subjects you focus on. While this can feel overwhelming, it can also be exciting to plan for your future and explore different possibilities.

---

3. Why Change Feels Stressful

3.1 Fear of the Unknown

A big part of change-related stress is not knowing what lies ahead. If you are switching schools, you might worry about making new friends or understanding new teachers' expectations. If you are starting a new job, you might not know if you will meet the performance standards. This uncertainty can create anxiety because people generally like feeling in control.

3.2 Attachment to the Familiar

Humans grow comfortable in routines. When change disrupts your normal pattern—like a new family schedule or a friend moving away—you lose the comfort of what you already know. It can feel unsettling, even if the change might eventually bring good outcomes.

3.3 Worry About Judgment

When you enter a new social group or try something different, you might fear how others will see you. Teens often face a lot of peer pressure and can be sensitive to acceptance. This worry can intensify feelings of anxiety or make you second-guess your decisions.

3.4 Emotional Overload

Changes can pile up. Maybe you are dealing with physical changes, emotional changes, and family transitions all at once. The cumulative effect can be overwhelming, causing stress or mood swings. Recognizing how these factors overlap can help you manage them more effectively.

---

4. Mindset Shifts That Help with Change

4.1 Viewing Change as Growth

Change is not always bad. Often, growth cannot happen without change. For example, entering a higher grade can challenge you academically, helping you build new skills. Moving to a new place can expand your perspective. By consciously reminding yourself that change can lead to positive developments, you can replace fear with cautious optimism.

4.2 Staying Open-Minded

An open mind helps you adapt more easily. If you approach a new situation with the attitude "I hate this," you block yourself from seeing potential benefits. Instead, try telling yourself, "Let's see what I can learn or enjoy in this situation." This does not mean ignoring valid fears, but it does mean giving the new scenario a fair chance.

4.3 Emphasizing Control Where Possible

While you cannot control everything, you can control some aspects of how you react. For example, if your family moves, you cannot stop the move, but you can decide how to set up your new room or which clubs to join at the new school. Focusing on areas you can influence reduces feelings of helplessness and increases confidence.

4.4 Patience with Yourself

Adapting to change takes time. You might expect to feel comfortable right away, but emotional adjustments can be slower. Give yourself permission to feel uneasy or anxious at first. Over a few weeks or months, you might realize you have grown used to the new arrangement. Patience helps you avoid harsh self-criticism during the transition period.

---

5. Strategies for Handling Physical Changes

5.1 Educate Yourself

If you are unsure why certain bodily changes are happening, look for reliable information. Health websites for teens, guidance from a trusted adult, or reputable books can help you understand the normal range of development. Knowing that what you are going through is common can reduce anxiety and embarrassment.

5.2 Focus on Self-Care

Healthy habits like balanced meals, enough sleep, and some form of exercise can help your body adjust more comfortably. Also, pay attention to personal hygiene. If you are dealing with skin changes, hair growth, or other shifts, consider talking to a healthcare provider or a trusted mentor for advice on suitable products or routines.

5.3 Dressing for Comfort and Confidence

Your body might not fit clothes the way it used to, or you might feel self-conscious about certain features. Choosing outfits that feel comfortable and reflect your personal style can boost your confidence. You do not have to follow every fashion trend—wear what makes you feel good and suits your changing shape.

5.4 Positive Body Talk

Avoid comparing your body to unrealistic images on social media or magazines. Everyone's development timeline is different. Practice saying supportive statements to yourself. For example, "My body is unique and is allowed to grow at its own pace," or "I deserve respect, no matter my size or shape." Positive thinking can help shift your mindset from self-criticism to self-acceptance.

---

6. Coping with Emotional Ups and Downs

6.1 Identify Your Emotions

When you feel a rush of sadness, anger, or anxiety, pause and name the emotion. Simply saying, "I feel sad because my friend moved away," can clarify what is happening. This awareness is the first step toward finding ways to handle it.

6.2 Healthy Outlets

If stress or sadness builds up, letting it out in safe ways can help. Some teens journal their worries, others talk to a close friend, and some engage in physical activities like running or dancing to burn off tension. Find a method that helps you release pent-up feelings so they do not linger and grow.

6.3 Consider Professional Help

If your emotional changes become overwhelming—like constant sadness, panic attacks, or harmful thoughts—do not hesitate to talk to a school counselor or mental health professional. They are trained to help you navigate the complex feelings associated with teenage changes, and seeking help early can prevent bigger issues later.

6.4 Build Emotional Resilience

Emotional resilience is your ability to bounce back from tough situations. You develop it by facing smaller challenges and learning from them. Each time you overcome a setback—like a bad grade or a fight with a friend—you become better at handling the next emotional hurdle. Embrace these experiences as lessons that strengthen your coping skills.

---

7. Facing Social Changes

7.1 Friendships Evolving

It can hurt when you drift apart from old friends. But as you discover new interests, you might find different circles of people who share your values. This natural process of changing friendships is common in adolescence. Appreciate the good memories with old friends while remaining open to forming new bonds.

7.2 Meeting New People

Whether it is a new school or a new club, meeting people can feel intimidating. Start with small steps—join group activities, sit with someone who seems approachable, or ask casual questions about their interests. Friendships do not form overnight, but consistent friendliness and genuine curiosity about others can lead to connections.

7.3 Handling Peer Pressure

In new social settings, you might face pressure to behave or dress in certain ways to fit in. Keep your own boundaries and identity in mind. If something goes against your comfort or values, politely decline. True friends will respect your choices rather than demand that you change who you are.

7.4 Family Relationship Shifts

As you grow older, your role in the family may change. Parents might grant you more responsibilities or freedoms, which can feel both exciting and stressful. If you disagree with a family rule, calmly explain your perspective and be open to compromise. Aim for mutual respect—your family likely wants what is best for you, even if you do not always see eye to eye.

---

8. Dealing with Academic or Future Changes

8.1 Course Load Increases

Transitioning to higher grades often means tougher courses and heavier homework. Keep track of due dates with a planner or app. Break large projects into smaller steps to avoid last-minute panic. If you feel overwhelmed, talk to your teachers—they can offer advice or adjust expectations if you are truly struggling.

8.2 Choosing a Path

By high school, you might sense pressure to decide on a future career or college major. Remember, it is okay not to have everything figured out. Exploring interests can guide you, but your path might shift later. Focus on gaining a variety of skills, staying curious, and doing your best in the present.

8.3 Setting Realistic Goals

If you plan to apply to competitive programs or scholarships, it is easy to feel stressed. Set smaller goals—like improving your grade in a certain subject this semester—rather than aiming for perfection in all areas. Celebrate progress along the way. Achieving these short-term goals can keep your morale high.

8.4 Seeking Guidance

School counselors, teachers, and even older students can offer tips on managing academic or career decisions. Ask about elective choices, extracurriculars, or internships that align with your potential interests. Hearing different viewpoints can reduce confusion and help you see the bigger picture.

---

9. Practical Approaches to Change Management

9.1 Making a Pros and Cons List

For a major life change—like switching schools or deciding whether to join a certain program—write down the positives and negatives. This gives you a clearer perspective instead of relying on vague worries. If the pros outweigh the cons, you might feel more confident about moving forward.

9.2 Creating a Flexible Plan

When you know change is coming, plan in small steps. If you are switching schools, research the new school's clubs or layout so you know where the cafeteria or library is. If you are moving to a new city, map out potential places to hang out. A plan lowers anxiety by giving you some structure.

9.3 Talking It Out

Share your concerns with someone you trust—like a friend, family member, or mentor. Verbalizing your thoughts can help you process them. Sometimes, they might offer solutions you never considered. Even if they do not have all the answers, a sympathetic ear can ease the emotional burden.

9.4 Visualization of Success

Spend a few moments picturing yourself handling the new situation well. For instance, imagine walking confidently into a new class, greeting people, and doing your best. Visualization is not magic, but it can mentally prepare you for positive action and reduce the fear that tries to hold you back.

---

10. Accepting the Emotional Roller Coaster

10.1 Normalizing Mixed Feelings

It is okay to feel excited, nervous, and sad all at once. For example, if you are moving to a better neighborhood, you might feel thrilled about meeting new people but upset about leaving old friends. Acknowledging these mixed emotions as normal prevents you from feeling guilty about having them.

10.2 Processing Loss

Change often involves losing something—like a familiar routine or a sense of stability. Even if the change leads to something better, give yourself time to mourn what is left behind. This might mean writing a goodbye note to your old bedroom or having a small farewell gathering with friends. Rituals like these can ease the sense of loss.

10.3 Avoiding Numbness

Sometimes, teens try to suppress emotions to cope with big changes. While bottling up feelings may work temporarily, it can lead to stronger outbursts later. Allow yourself to cry if you need to, or talk about your concerns. Expressing emotions is a sign of strength, not weakness, because it lets you handle them in a healthier way.

10.4 Finding Moments of Joy

During periods of transition, do not forget to seek small joys. Watch a comedy show, bake cookies, or do a quick craft. These moments of lightness can balance out the heavier emotions. Even if it feels like life is in chaos, bits of happiness can remind you that not everything is turning upside down.

---

11. When Change Becomes Overwhelming

11.1 Signs of Severe Stress

If you are having trouble sleeping, losing interest in activities you used to love, or noticing significant shifts in your appetite, it might be more than typical stress. Feeling constant dread, frequent headaches, or recurring stomach issues can also signal high anxiety levels. Pay attention to these signs and take them seriously.

11.2 Reaching Out for Help

Do not hesitate to approach a school counselor, teacher, or medical professional if the stress becomes too heavy. You can also call hotlines or look for online counseling services if you feel you cannot talk to people around you. Admitting that you need help is a brave choice that can guide you toward useful resources.

11.3 Creating a Support System

Even if professional help is not easily available, building a network of friends, relatives, or mentors you can trust is crucial. Let them know you are going through a tough transition. They may offer emotional support, solutions, or simply a safe space to share how you feel.

11.4 Self-Compassion

In moments when you feel overwhelmed, treat yourself kindly. Avoid harsh self-criticism like, "I should be over this by now," or "I'm weak for feeling this way." Show the same empathy to yourself that you would to a friend facing a tough time. Encouraging words in your own mind can make a significant difference.

---

12. Real-Life Examples of Dealing with Change

12.1 Priya's Move to a New City

Priya had lived in the same town her whole life. When her parents announced they were moving across the country, she felt devastated. She feared losing her best friend and not fitting in at the new school. To ease the transition, Priya made a small plan: she researched her new city's highlights, joined a few online groups for local teens, and promised her best friend they would video chat every weekend. Although the first few weeks were tough, Priya ended up discovering an art club at her new school that she loved. She kept in touch with her old friend, and gradually, she found her footing in the new city.

12.2 James's Switch from Sports to Drama

James was known as a soccer player, but after an injury, he realized he could not keep up with the sport. He felt lost because soccer had defined so much of his identity. With encouragement from a teacher, he decided to audition for the school play—something he had never considered. At first, he felt awkward and uncertain. But as he got into rehearsals, he found that performing on stage allowed him a new sense of fulfillment. Though it was a big change in how peers saw him, James learned that his worth was not tied to one activity. He discovered new talents and made friends he might never have met otherwise.

12.3 Alina's Shift in Friend Group

Alina had a tight-knit friend circle throughout middle school. But in high school, she noticed they all wanted to party while she preferred quieter hangouts and academic clubs. Over time, she felt out of place. She gradually spent more time with classmates from her debate club. While it was painful to drift from her old friends, Alina recognized that it was a natural progression. She stayed polite with her old circle but found deeper connections with people who shared her interests. Accepting this social change, rather than forcing old friendships to stay the same, gave her a healthier sense of belonging.

12.4 Malik's Home Life Change

Malik's parents got divorced, and he had to split his time between two households. This major change disrupted his usual routines. Initially, he felt anger and confusion. He reached out to a school counselor who helped him express his feelings constructively. Malik also set up a consistent schedule—on which days he would be at each parent's house—and made sure he had duplicates of key items, like phone chargers and toiletries, so he would not feel disorganized. Over time, he adapted, and while the situation was not ideal, the structured plan and emotional support eased his stress.

---

13. Practical Exercises to Manage Change

13.1 Emotion Check-In

Once a day, set aside a few minutes to label your mood: Are you anxious, excited, sad, or calm? Write it in a journal or a note on your phone. Then note what might be causing that feeling. Over time, you will see patterns—what triggers stress or joy—and can adjust your coping strategies accordingly.

13.2 Resilience Reminder List

Create a list of times you overcame challenges. For example, "I made new friends at camp last year," or "I handled a tough math test and did okay." Keep this list visible or on your phone. When a new change makes you nervous, look at your list to remind yourself you have handled tough situations before.

13.3 Visualization of Positive Outcomes

Pick a specific change that worries you—a new school, a new friend group, or a new job. Close your eyes and imagine a successful scenario. Picture yourself navigating the first day calmly, saying hello to someone, or completing a new task well. Focus on the details—how you look, the environment, the feeling of relief afterward. This mental practice can ease nerves and boost your confidence when the real situation happens.

13.4 Timed Worry Session

Set a timer for 5 or 10 minutes when you allow yourself to worry about the upcoming change. Write down or speak aloud all your fears. Once the timer is up, stop and do something uplifting—like listening to music or talking to a positive friend. This technique confines worries to a small window, preventing them from taking over your whole day.

Chapter 19: Spreading Confidence to Others

1. Introduction

Confidence is valuable not just for our own growth but also in how we interact with the people around us. When we believe in ourselves, we can lift others up too. Think about how great it feels when someone shows you kindness, believes in your ability, or supports you when you try something new. That person's confidence and encouragement can motivate you to aim higher.

In this chapter, we explore how teen girls can share confidence with friends, family, and even strangers. This might mean giving honest compliments, helping classmates with homework, or mentoring younger students at school. By doing so, you create a cycle of positivity. Each time you help someone feel more sure of themselves, you reinforce your own sense of worth. By the end, you will see that spreading confidence is not about being perfect or bossy—it is about offering real support and warmth, which in turn strengthens your own self-esteem.

2. Why Share Confidence?

2.1 Building Positive Connections

When you encourage someone, you form or strengthen a bond. People feel safer around those who offer sincere praise and understanding. This can lead to lasting friendships, a better classroom environment, or a more supportive team. Over time, these positive connections expand, making your social circle a place where people help each other, rather than compete in harmful ways.

2.2 Boosting Your Own Self-Esteem

Confidence grows when you see the good effect of your words and actions on others. Suppose you reassure a friend who is nervous about a presentation. Later, she tells you she did well, partly because you made her believe she could succeed. Hearing that can remind you of your own power to do good. This, in turn, strengthens your belief in your own abilities.

2.3 Creating a Supportive Environment

Whether at home, in school, or in your community, a supportive environment makes life easier for everyone. If you set an example by being respectful, kind, and uplifting, others might copy these behaviors. Over time, this can transform a tense classroom or a divided friend group into a place where people look out for each other's well-being.

2.4 Spreading Hope

In a world where negativity can dominate social media or gossip, being a person who spreads confidence can feel refreshing and hopeful. A simple act, like cheering on a teammate, can do more than just help that individual. It can encourage anyone who sees it, reminding them that kindness and support still exist. Bit by bit, such gestures can lower the overall negativity around you.

---

3. Simple Ways to Encourage Others

3.1 Giving Compliments

Sincere compliments are a quick way to make someone's day better. Focus on specifics rather than general flattery. For example, if a classmate writes a great essay, say, "Your introduction really caught my attention, and your points are clear," instead of just "Good job." By pointing out something meaningful, you show you genuinely noticed their work.

3.2 Sharing Skills or Knowledge

If you are good at math, offer to help a friend who struggles with it. If you are skilled at public speaking, help classmates practice for their oral presentations. Teaching someone can boost their confidence in that subject and remind you of your own competence. It can also deepen your understanding of the topic.

3.3 Writing Notes of Appreciation

In the digital age, a handwritten note or card stands out. Send a short note to a teacher who supported you or a friend who was there for you. Expressing gratitude can make them feel recognized and valued. Even a brief message like, "Thank you for always listening when I need to talk," can mean a lot.

3.4 Celebrating Small Achievements

Big achievements—like winning a tournament or getting the top grade—often get noticed. But small achievements also deserve recognition. Maybe your friend managed to run one extra lap in P.E. or overcame her fear of speaking up in a group meeting. A small "I saw that and it was awesome!" can motivate them to keep improving.

---

4. Being a Role Model

4.1 Consistency in Behavior

If you want others to trust you and feel confident around you, your actions need to match your words. For instance, if you say you believe in kindness but often gossip or mock people, your message loses credibility. Strive for consistency: treat people with respect in both private and public settings. This steadiness shows integrity, which can inspire others to do the same.

4.2 Owning Mistakes

No one is perfect. If you slip up—maybe you lose your temper or break a promise—acknowledge it quickly and apologize if needed. Owning mistakes teaches others that being responsible is more important than saving face. It also shows you do not see yourself as above criticism, which can make people more comfortable around you.

4.3 Displaying Empathy

Empathy is about understanding and sharing someone else's feelings. If you notice a friend is upset, ask how they are and truly listen to their answer. Even if you cannot fix their problem, being there and offering genuine support can raise their confidence and help them feel less alone. When people see you acting with empathy, they often learn to do the same.

4.4 Staying Positive (Without Ignoring Reality)

Being positive does not mean pretending everything is fine when it is not. It means choosing to focus on what can be done rather than just listing what is wrong. If your group project is behind schedule, you can say, "We have challenges, but we still have time to divide the tasks and catch up," instead of "We are doomed." This realistic positivity can keep people motivated and less stressed.

---

5. Helping Friends Grow Confidently

5.1 Encouraging Them to Try New Things

Sometimes friends hesitate to try a new club, sport, or activity because they fear failure. A supportive nudge—like offering to go with them to the first meeting—can make a difference. By showing them that it is normal to experiment and learn, you help them adopt a mindset where they see challenges as fun opportunities instead of threats.

5.2 Listening Actively

If your friend is venting about a problem, avoid jumping straight into giving advice unless they ask for it. Often, people just want to be heard. Show you are listening by making eye contact, nodding, and asking clarifying questions. This makes them feel validated and can lead them to discover solutions on their own.

5.3 Sharing Your Own Struggles

Confidence does not grow from seeing someone act perfect. It often grows when you realize you are not alone in your struggles. If you are comfortable, share your own experiences with insecurity or challenges. This can reassure your friend that setbacks happen to everyone and that it is possible to move forward.

5.4 Setting Mutual Goals

If you and a friend both want to improve in a certain area—like fitness, a particular subject, or a creative hobby—you can set shared goals. For example, commit to studying math together twice a week or going for a jog on Saturday mornings. Holding each other accountable can be motivating, and when one of you hits a milestone, the other can celebrate that progress.

---

6. Supporting Younger Teens or Siblings

6.1 Mentoring and Guidance

If you have younger siblings or cousins, they might look up to you more than you realize. Offer simple lessons in tasks they find hard, whether it is organizing homework or dealing with school drama. A little guidance can prevent them from feeling lost. Also, sharing your experiences can help them see what might work best for them.

6.2 Teaching Skills

If you are adept at something—cooking a basic recipe, writing a resume for a part-time job, or any skill you have learned—show them how. This not only benefits them but also strengthens your own grasp of the skill through teaching. Confidence can be passed down like this: you show them it is doable, and they start believing in themselves.

6.3 Positive Reinforcement

Younger teens can be sensitive to criticism and might already face pressure at school. Offer sincere praise when they accomplish something, even if it seems small. For instance, if they took the initiative to study or handled a conflict maturely, acknowledge that. This can encourage more responsible behavior and self-trust.

6.4 Providing a Safe Space

Let them know they can come to you with questions or worries without being judged. Sometimes, younger teens feel they cannot talk to parents but might feel safer speaking to an older sibling or relative who is closer to their age. Being that safe person helps them develop confidence in handling problems, knowing they have support if needed.

---

7. Contributing in School and Community

7.1 Peer Tutoring

Many schools have peer-tutoring programs where you can help classmates who struggle with specific subjects. Volunteering as a tutor not only aids them academically but also boosts your own confidence, as you confirm your knowledge by teaching it. Plus, you learn communication and teaching skills that are valuable in any field.

7.2 Leading Group Projects with Kindness

If you are assigned the role of group leader, use it as a chance to uplift your teammates. Assign tasks fairly, listen to everyone's input, and step in to help if someone is stuck. This approach fosters a cooperative environment. When the project succeeds, everyone feels proud, and you have shown what positive leadership looks like.

7.3 Volunteering in Community Activities

Whether it is cleaning up a park, helping at a food drive, or reading to younger children in a library program, community service can spread confidence on a broader scale. People see young volunteers stepping up, which can inspire them. It also gives you a sense of accomplishment, reinforcing that your efforts matter.

7.4 Organizing Small Events

If you have time and support, consider organizing a small event—like a clothing swap, a charity fundraiser, or a mini-workshop on study tips. Gather a few friends to help. Bringing people together for a positive cause not only strengthens community ties but also demonstrates how a little initiative can create a ripple effect of confidence and unity.

---

8. Online Etiquette for Encouragement

8.1 Positive Comments and Messages

Social media can be harsh, but you can choose to make it better. If you see a friend post artwork or share an achievement, leave a meaningful comment. Say, "This is so creative! I love how you used color," or "I'm proud of you for finishing that project." Positive online feedback can offset the common negativity found on many platforms.

8.2 Avoiding Toxic Threads

Sometimes people get into heated arguments or negative discussions online. Jumping in can fuel more negativity. If you feel strongly about an issue, you can still express your view, but try to stay calm and factual. Or simply remove yourself from toxic threads. Preserving your own mental well-being also keeps you in a better place to spread confidence in other interactions.

8.3 Sharing Useful Content

If you come across an inspiring article, a scholarship link, or a motivational video, share it with those who might benefit. Being a source of helpful information can raise others' confidence because you provide resources they might not have found on their own. This is a simple way to let friends know you think of their interests.

8.4 Respecting Boundaries

While encouraging others online, also respect their privacy. If someone is dealing with a personal problem, do not push them to discuss it publicly. Offer a private message or let them know you are there if they need to talk. This respectful stance shows others that your help comes with understanding and trust.

---

9. Handling Resistance or Negativity

9.1 Recognizing Some Are Not Ready

Not everyone welcomes encouragement. Some people might be cynical or stuck in a negative mindset. If you offer kind words and they respond with sarcasm, remember it might reflect their own struggles. You cannot force someone to accept your support. Do not take it personally—stay polite, and move on without blaming yourself.

9.2 Setting Boundaries

Sharing confidence should not mean letting people take advantage of you. If someone constantly puts you down or uses your kindness in manipulative ways, step back. You can still be polite, but limit the time or energy you spend on them. Your well-being matters, and it is hard to uplift others when they consistently drain your positivity.

9.3 Knowing When to Seek Help

If a friend's negativity or personal struggles are severe—such as showing signs of self-harm or dangerous behavior—encouraging words alone may not be enough. Talk to a trusted adult, counselor, or teacher about the situation. It is not a betrayal to ask for professional help when you see someone possibly at risk.

9.4 Staying True to Your Values

Even if others laugh at your attempts to be supportive, do not let that discourage you. If you know in your heart that being kind and uplifting is the right choice, stand by it. Over time, some who mocked you may change their view, or you might inspire a few quiet observers who decide to follow your example.

---

10. The Power of Small Acts

10.1 Random Acts of Kindness

Simple gestures—like holding the door for someone carrying books, offering a seat to someone tired, or sending an anonymous positive note—can leave a mark. These small acts show that you notice others and care about their well-being. Over time, people remember these gestures, and it can encourage them to act similarly.

10.2 Compliment Chains

Some teens create a "compliment box" at school, where students can drop in notes praising a classmate's achievement or kindness. These notes are then distributed. Or, in a group chat, you can start a chain by tagging a person and praising one good thing about them. That person then praises someone else, and so on. It can shift the group's tone from criticism to warmth.

10.3 Sharing Inspirational Quotes or Stories

A well-timed motivational quote or short story of someone overcoming challenges can give a friend a fresh perspective. This does not mean spamming people with endless quotes. However, sending an uplifting text when you sense your friend is down can remind them that hope is out there.

10.4 Following Through

If you promise to help someone, do your best to keep that promise. Whether it is practicing lines for a play together or reviewing their resume before a job fair, following through shows reliability. It reassures others that you are someone they can trust, which is crucial in building an environment where confidence can flourish.

---

11. Confidence Building Activities in Groups

11.1 Group Praise Circles

In some clubs or youth groups, people sit in a circle and take turns saying something positive about each member. This might sound awkward at first, but it often ends up being very meaningful. Hearing direct praise from peers can have a big effect on self-esteem. It also challenges participants to find genuine compliments, strengthening the group's overall morale.

11.2 Team-Building Exercises

Games where members must cooperate—like a puzzle-solving task or a scavenger hunt—can teach people to support each other. By pointing out each person's strengths ("You are good at spotting clues," "You are great at leading the group"), you embed a sense of value in every participant. Over time, this fosters a more trusting team culture.

11.3 Public Speaking Workshops

Encouraging a friend to join you in a short speech or presentation can help both of you tackle any fear of public speaking. After each attempt, exchange constructive feedback, focusing on what the speaker did well before suggesting areas of improvement. Applauding each other's progress can lift confidence levels in a shared way.

11.4 Group Reflection

At the end of a project or semester, gather friends or classmates to reflect on what went right and how each person contributed. This reflection can highlight accomplishments people might have overlooked. For instance, maybe someone was the peacemaker during conflicts or someone else provided creative solutions. Recognizing these acts ensures that everyone sees their role as important.

---

12. Spreading Confidence Beyond School

12.1 Neighborhood Initiatives

Look around your neighborhood for small ways to help. Maybe you can organize a book exchange shelf where neighbors share used books. Or gather a few teens to help an elderly neighbor with yard work. Each act of community service can inspire neighbors to trust teens more and can encourage them to do their own acts of kindness.

12.2 Online Communities

Beyond social media for friends, there are online forums for shared interests—be it music production, fan clubs, or craft exchanges. Participating in these communities by giving constructive feedback or sharing free resources can encourage people worldwide. You might never meet them in person, but your supportive input can still boost someone's confidence far away.

12.3 Leading Workshops or Camps

If you feel skilled in a certain area—like painting, coding, or dance—look into organizing a mini-workshop or a short summer camp for younger kids at a local community center. Teaching them the basics and showing them they can learn can ignite their confidence. This also cements your own mastery and leadership skills.

12.4 Helping Local Organizations

Many charities or nonprofits run on volunteers. If you join a campaign (like raising funds for animal shelters or supporting literacy programs), your involvement can encourage the organization's members. Seeing a teen dedicate time and skills can lift the spirits of those who have been working in challenging conditions, and your enthusiasm might draw other young volunteers.

---

13. Balancing Self-Care While Uplifting Others

13.1 Avoiding Burnout

Supporting others can be draining if you forget your own limits. Continuously helping friends with emotional issues or tutoring too many classmates can eat into your rest time or personal needs. Learn to say no when you need a break or have too many commitments. A burned-out helper can accidentally lose patience or bring down the mood, defeating the purpose of spreading confidence.

13.2 Setting Boundaries

Some people might rely on you too heavily once they see your supportive nature. While it is wonderful to help, you are not responsible for solving everyone's problems. Politely clarify what you can and cannot do. For instance, "I can help with your project for an hour tonight, but then I need to focus on my own assignment."

13.3 Checking Your Own Emotions

Encouragement should feel good, not forced. If you start to resent someone or feel obligated to help them constantly, it might be time to reassess that relationship. A healthy dynamic has give-and-take, where both parties understand each other's boundaries and reciprocate support in some form.

13.4 Finding Mentors or Confidants

Just as you help others, you may need someone to inspire you—a friend, older sibling, teacher, or counselor. Make sure you have a source of encouragement when you feel depleted. Talking about your experiences in uplifting others can help you learn new approaches and avoid emotional strain.

---

14. Cultural and Social Sensitivity

14.1 Respecting Differences

When encouraging someone, be mindful of cultural or personal norms. Some families do not value public praise, preferring private compliments. Others might have different views on what success means. Listening and observing can help you tailor your support so it is received well.

14.2 Avoiding Stereotypes

Do not assume you know what people need based on stereotypes about gender, ethnicity, or background. Ask questions: "How can I help?" or "What kind of support do you find most useful?" This approach ensures you do not unintentionally offend or diminish someone's experience.

14.3 Language Matters

Certain words or phrases can uplift, while others can unintentionally hurt. Avoid labeling people in a negative way, even if it is meant as a joke. Instead, use language that acknowledges effort and potential. Saying, "You worked hard on this," is often more empowering than, "You're a genius," which suggests talent is everything and discourages trying when faced with difficulties.

14.4 Learning from Diverse Perspectives

Sharing confidence is also about learning from others. If you see someone from a different culture or background succeeding in a context that is new to you, ask them how they overcame obstacles. By showing genuine interest in their story, you both build confidence in each other's abilities and experiences.

---

15. Long-Term Impact of Spreading Confidence

15.1 Strengthening Friendships

When your friend knows you are genuinely on their side, they are more likely to trust you with their worries and triumphs. This trust can turn casual acquaintances into deep bonds. Years later, you might look back and see that your honest encouragement during a tough time was a turning point for them.

15.2 Influencing Younger Generations

If you mentor younger teens, they might grow up remembering how you treated them. In turn, they could mentor others one day. This passing down of supportive behavior can shape communities in ways you might never fully see but can be proud of knowing you started something positive.

15.3 Expanding Opportunities

Sometimes helping others can open unexpected doors. Perhaps a teacher notices your leadership style and recommends you for a student council role. Or a friend you encouraged might invite you to a future event or program because they value your supportive nature. Being known as someone who builds others up can attract good opportunities.

15.4 Personal Growth

The more you share confidence, the more you refine qualities like patience, empathy, and creativity in solving problems. Over time, this personal growth can reflect in your own achievements—academic or otherwise. People who uplift others often discover new strengths within themselves.

---

16. Real-Life Stories: Confidence Shared

16.1 Aisha's Lunch Table Initiative

Aisha noticed that some classmates had no one to sit with at lunch. She decided to start a "welcoming table" in the cafeteria. She invited anyone who felt alone to join. Over time, that table became a friendly spot where students talked about common interests. Some who initially sat there quietly eventually opened up and found new friends. This simple idea spread confidence because it showed no one had to be alone, and everyone's presence was valued.

16.2 Daniel's Peer Mentoring

Daniel struggled with reading in elementary school, but by high school, he had improved a lot thanks to a teacher who spent extra time with him. Wanting to give back, Daniel volunteered to read with younger students who found reading challenging. He shared tips that helped him and praised their small steps. Many of those kids reported feeling less embarrassed about reading, and some even began enjoying books. Daniel's empathy, shaped by his own past struggles, helped others believe in their potential.

16.3 Tia's Dance Club Support

Tia led the dance club at her school. Instead of picking only the best dancers for performances, she encouraged beginners to join and taught them basics. Whenever someone nailed a new move, Tia made sure the whole club clapped. This routine recognized progress, not just final perfection. As a result, more students felt confident signing up, and the club's team spirit soared.

16.4 Mira's Online Project

Mira loved coding and set up a small website offering free lessons for kids on basic computer programming. She also created a forum section where learners could post questions, and she or other teen volunteers would answer. Over time, many kids who learned on the site started answering each other's questions. This peer-driven confidence cycle showed how one person's initiative in a digital space can spark a whole community of support.

---

17. Practical Exercises for Spreading Confidence

17.1 Compliment Challenge

Pick one day each week to give at least three sincere compliments to people around you. Note how they react. Keep doing it for a month.

Observe if this changes the mood in your class or friend group. Reflect on how it makes you feel as well.

17.2 Shared Study Session

Gather a small group of classmates, especially those who might be struggling in a subject you know well. Offer a casual study session—maybe once a week—where you go over notes, solve problems together, and share strategies. Track any improvements in their test scores or participation, and notice how your own understanding might also deepen.

17.3 Gratitude Board

Create or suggest a "gratitude board" in a common area—like a hallway or a classroom bulletin board—where students can pin notes praising a classmate or thanking someone for help. Periodically read them and see how it lifts the overall environment.

17.4 Community Chain Reaction

Plan a small volunteer project with friends—such as picking up trash at a local park or collecting canned goods for a food pantry. At the end of the activity, invite participants to share what they learned or how they felt making a difference. Encourage them to pass on the goodwill by organizing their own mini project next time. Monitor if it sparks more community involvement.

Chapter 20: Building a Bright Future

1. Introduction

You have spent the previous chapters learning to understand yourself, develop communication skills, build self-care habits, manage stress, and even pass on confidence to others. Now comes the question: What next? The teenage years are a foundation for the rest of your life, but they are also a time of possibilities. Laying out a general plan for the future can help you feel secure, even if the details are still being figured out.

This final chapter looks at how to maintain everything you have learned—self-belief, emotional balance, healthy habits—and use them as cornerstones for adulthood. We will explore how to set long-term goals, keep adjusting them, and stay resilient when life throws unexpected challenges. By the end, you should have a clearer sense that building a bright future is not about a perfect path. Rather, it involves staying flexible, harnessing your strengths, and believing you have the capability to move forward even when times get tough.

2. Keeping Your Confidence Growth Alive

2.1 Reviewing Past Lessons

Confidence is not a one-time achievement—it needs regular upkeep. It can help to revisit the lessons you have learned in this book. Skim through the sections on handling doubt, setting boundaries, or practicing mindfulness. Sometimes, when life gets chaotic, a quick refresher can remind you of strategies that worked in the past.

2.2 Tracking Progress

One practical method is to note your achievements or improvements every few months. This can be as simple as writing a short diary entry: "Things I accomplished this season." By reflecting on how you handled difficult situations or overcame personal challenges, you reinforce the idea that you are capable of dealing with new hurdles. This record also becomes a source of inspiration whenever you feel stuck.

2.3 Staying Realistic

Confidence does not mean pretending you never have weaknesses. It is about recognizing that you can handle and improve them. Keep your view balanced: celebrate your strengths while acknowledging areas that need growth. This genuine self-awareness stops you from being overconfident or underestimating yourself.

2.4 Surrounding Yourself with Positive Influences

The people you frequently interact with can affect how you see yourself. Seek out friends, mentors, or online communities that value your well-being. Avoid or minimize contact with those who constantly criticize or drain you. A supportive network can keep your self-confidence intact and push you to keep moving forward.

---

3. Setting Long-Term Goals

3.1 Benefits of Having a Vision

Having an idea of where you want to go—whether it is academically, professionally, or personally—gives you motivation. Waking up each day feels more purposeful when you have small steps leading to a bigger target. You do not need to map out every detail of your life, but identifying a direction can make decisions easier along the way.

3.2 Types of Long-Term Goals

- **Academic Goals:** E.g., aiming for a certain GPA, planning to get into a specific college or a particular major.

- **Career Goals:** E.g., considering industries you might want to explore, like healthcare, tech, teaching, or the arts.
- **Skill Development:** E.g., wanting to become fluent in a new language, learn advanced coding, or excel in a musical instrument.
- **Personal Growth:** E.g., working on patience, improving public speaking, or traveling to broaden your perspective.

3.3 Breaking Goals into Steps

A long-term goal can feel intimidating. For instance, "I want to become a nurse" might involve multiple steps: researching nursing programs, excelling in science classes, volunteering at a hospital, and applying to colleges. Outline these steps in a timeline—what can you do this year, next year, and so on. This structure turns daunting tasks into manageable actions.

3.4 Revisiting and Revising

As you learn more about the world and about yourself, your goals might shift. Maybe you realize you prefer environmental science over medicine. That is fine. Check in every few months or once a year: Are your goals still relevant? Have new interests emerged? Adjust accordingly, knowing that change is not failure but a sign of growth.

---

4. Maintaining Healthy Habits

4.1 Physical Health as a Priority

Continuing regular exercise, sleep routines, and balanced eating can set you up for a strong adulthood. If you let these habits slide when stress increases—like during exams—you might find your energy and focus drop. Keep a basic schedule: aim for 7–9 hours of sleep, choose nutritious meals most of the time, and find a form of movement you like. These steps lay the foundation for well-being.

4.2 Ongoing Self-Care

Self-care is not just for times of crisis. Keep doing small actions like short mindfulness breaks, journaling, or creative outlets. Treat these routines as important appointments with yourself. Even as you take on bigger responsibilities—like part-time jobs or leadership roles—self-care prevents burnout and helps you stay balanced.

4.3 Emotional Check-Ins

Regularly ask yourself how you are feeling. If you notice you are often moody or stressed, figure out what might be causing it—lack of sleep, too many extracurriculars, or tension at home. Once identified, take steps to fix or manage the root cause. Consistent emotional awareness stops problems from piling up.

4.4 Keeping Boundaries Strong

As you progress to higher studies, workplaces, or new social circles, people may try to push your boundaries. Maybe a college friend wants you to party every night or a boss demands extra shifts beyond your capacity. Remember that saying no is still valid. Protect your personal space, mental health, and time. This helps you remain centered and confident about your choices.

---

5. Building Financial Skills and Independence

5.1 Basic Budgeting

Even if you only earn allowance or make a little money from babysitting, start practicing budgeting. Figure out how much you save, how much you spend on personal treats, and how much you might invest in future plans. Learning to track expenses early can prevent financial stress later on.

5.2 Earning Opportunities

A part-time job, freelance gigs, or summer work can teach you valuable lessons. Beyond the money earned, you gain work ethic, time management, and a deeper sense of responsibility. You might also discover new skills or fields you enjoy. Keep an eye out for internships or volunteer roles that align with your interests.

5.3 Understanding Credit and Debt

While you might not use credit cards yet, learning the basics of interest rates, loans, and credit scores can be helpful. Talk to a trusted adult or read simple articles online about responsible credit use. This knowledge can help you avoid mistakes—like racking up high-interest debt in college.

5.4 Planning for the Future

If you aim to attend college or vocational training, start looking at scholarship opportunities early. Learn about grants, student loan basics, and ways to minimize debt. Even if college is a few years away, awareness of these options can shape your high school decisions—like aiming for good grades or joining certain extracurriculars that improve scholarship chances.

---

6. Managing Relationships as You Grow Older

6.1 Evolving Friendships

Your friends might scatter to different schools or even move to new cities. While physical distance can be challenging, use technology to stay in touch if the friendship is meaningful. Also, remain open to forming new connections in your new environments. Long-lasting friendships adapt to changes, but that requires effort from both sides.

6.2 Maintaining Family Bonds

As you become more independent, conflicts with family might arise around rules, curfews, or lifestyle choices. Communicating your needs calmly and respecting their concerns can help. Negotiate solutions that consider both your growing autonomy and their sense of responsibility. This mutual respect can strengthen family relationships over time.

6.3 Navigating Romantic Connections

In later teen years or early adulthood, romantic relationships might become a bigger focus. Keep in mind what you learned about boundaries, respect, and self-care. A healthy partnership should bring growth, not stifle it. Ensure that both you and your partner encourage each other's goals. If a relationship undermines your confidence or well-being, it may be time to reassess it.

6.4 Professional Networking

As you start exploring jobs, internships, or college clubs, professional or academic networking becomes relevant. This might mean talking to professors, attending career fairs, or asking professionals about their fields. Even if you do not feel "professional" yet, building polite relationships can open doors in the future. Confidence in these interactions signals you take yourself seriously, which can impress potential mentors or employers.

---

7. Balancing Freedom and Responsibility

7.1 Enjoying Your Independence

As you get older, you may gain freedoms like choosing your own schedule, managing your finances, or traveling without adult supervision. Use these freedoms wisely. Embrace the opportunities to make your own decisions, try new things, and shape your identity. However, remember that independence is linked to responsibility.

7.2 Accepting Consequences

Part of growing up is dealing with outcomes, good or bad, from your decisions. If you miss a deadline, you might lose points or face criticism. This does not make you a failure—it is a learning opportunity. Reflect on what went wrong and how to fix it next time. Owning up to mistakes can deepen your confidence in your ability to handle life's complexities.

7.3 Time Management in Adulthood

Your schedule might become even busier with college classes, part-time work, or full-time job responsibilities. Techniques you learned as a teen—like using planners, setting priorities, or breaking tasks into steps—will remain crucial. Maintaining these habits helps you juggle multiple commitments without constant stress.

7.4 Knowing Your Limits

With new freedoms, you might face peer or societal pressure to party, spend, or commit to too many activities. Always remember the boundary-setting skills from earlier chapters. If you are exhausted or uncomfortable, it is okay to say no. Protecting your well-being is part of being a responsible, confident young adult.

---

8. Continuing Education and Lifelong Learning

8.1 College, Vocational School, or Other Paths

Not everyone follows the same path after high school. Some go to four-year universities, others join community colleges, apprenticeships, or direct work. Research the options. Consider how each aligns with your interests and goals. Confidence in your choice comes from knowing you have explored multiple routes and picked one that suits you best.

8.2 Embracing Curiosity

Even after formal education, keep learning. Attend workshops, read books in areas you find fascinating, or take online courses for personal development. This ongoing learning keeps your mind sharp and can lead you to discover new hobbies or career shifts later in life. Curiosity also helps you adapt in a fast-changing world.

8.3 Self-Directed Projects

Whether it is writing a blog, launching a small business, or learning a new language on your own, self-directed projects build confidence. They teach you problem-solving and time management in a real-world context. Having a portfolio of such projects can also impress future employers or college admissions.

8.4 Mentoring Others in Learning

Share your knowledge with peers or younger students. This reinforces your own understanding and enhances your leadership skills. Teaching someone else also keeps you humble, because you remember how tough it can be to learn something new, which in turn increases your empathy and approachability.

---

9. Staying Resilient Through Change

9.1 Preparing for Life's Twists

Adulthood brings its own transitions: relocating for work, managing finances, or dealing with unexpected events like health issues. Recognize that uncertainty is part of life. Confidence does not remove challenges; it helps you handle them more calmly. Maintain the strategies that worked in your teens—like mindfulness, self-care, and problem-solving steps.

9.2 Emotional Flexibility

When faced with disappointment—like a job rejection or a tough semester—emotional flexibility means allowing yourself to feel sadness or frustration but also knowing you can move forward. Give yourself time to recover, then look for alternative routes or new chances. This skill can keep you from getting stuck in defeat.

9.3 Keeping Support Networks

Friends and mentors may change, but you can actively cultivate new relationships. Join professional groups, reconnect with old classmates, or keep in touch with family who encourage you. A strong support network makes it easier to bounce back when life throws curveballs.

9.4 Celebrating Milestones

As you reach certain life events—graduations, promotions, personal achievements—take a moment to acknowledge them. Reflect on the effort you invested and the hurdles you overcame. This reflection can fuel your motivation for the next phase. It also provides a sense of continuity between your teen years and adult successes.

---

10. Giving Back to the Community

10.1 Volunteering as an Adult

Volunteer work can remain a constant in your life, whether you are in college or working. You might choose causes aligned with your interests—like mental health, education, or environmental protection. Volunteering lets you meet people from different backgrounds and strengthens your sense of purpose.

10.2 Mentoring Younger Students

If you go to college or enter a profession, consider mentoring teens who want to follow a similar path. Share tips on scholarships, study habits, or job opportunities. This cycle of guidance ensures that each generation benefits from the wisdom of those who walked the path before them, much like how you once received help or advice.

10.3 Community Leadership

Look for ways to be a leader in your neighborhood or workplace, like organizing social or health initiatives. Leadership does not require a fancy title—it can be as simple as starting a local clean-up drive. Taking on such roles enhances your confidence, communication skills, and sense of civic responsibility.

10.4 Encouraging Civic Engagement

Staying informed about local issues, voting when eligible, and voicing your opinions responsibly can shape the community and the future of your region or country. Encouraging your peers to do the same amplifies the effect. Being civically engaged shows that you believe your actions matter, a core principle of sustained confidence.

---

11. Tools and Resources for Your Future

11.1 Career Centers and Counselors

If you enroll in college or vocational programs, take advantage of career centers. They offer resume advice, mock interviews, and information on internships. Even if you are not sure about your future path, they can help you explore possibilities. High school counselors can also guide you in picking the right courses or extracurriculars that align with your potential interests.

11.2 Online Platforms

Websites like LinkedIn let you network with professionals, search job postings, and follow companies you find interesting. You can also join online forums or groups that match your career goals or passions. Just ensure your online profile remains professional if you aim to connect with future employers or mentors.

11.3 E-Learning Websites

Platforms offering free or low-cost courses—like edX, Coursera, or Khan Academy—can enhance your knowledge outside of formal schooling. If you ever feel stuck or curious about a topic, you can quickly access tutorials or structured courses. This approach keeps you learning throughout your life, reinforcing your ability to adapt to changing fields.

11.4 Personal Development Apps

Some apps focus on time management, habit tracking, or mental health. They can remind you to stick to goals—like reading daily, practicing a language, or doing quick workout sessions. By integrating these apps into your routine, you maintain the self-discipline gained in your teen years, ensuring your confidence and efficiency grow.

---

12. Overcoming Post-Teen Challenges

12.1 Transition to College or Work

Leaving the familiar environment of high school can be a big shift. You might face more academic competition, more self-managed schedules, or the pressures of paying bills. However, the self-confidence you developed as a teen can carry over. Remember the basics: break tasks down, seek support when needed, and believe in your capacity to learn.

12.2 Living Independently

If you move out to live on campus or rent a place, tasks like cooking, cleaning, and budgeting become your responsibility. While it can be overwhelming at first, approach it as a practical exercise. Each day is a chance to refine your life skills. Give yourself patience—no one masters independence instantly.

12.3 Relationship Boundaries

Adult life may bring new dating dynamics, workplace interactions, or friendships with older individuals. Keep your boundaries, communication skills, and respect for others intact. Maturity often involves standing your ground while understanding others' perspectives. This balance can save you from toxic situations and foster healthier connections.

12.4 Handling Career Doubts

It is normal to question your chosen path after a few semesters or a couple of years in the workforce. If uncertainty arises, revisit your strengths and interests. Talk to mentors or career counselors. Sometimes a minor shift—like changing your specialization or transferring to a different role—can rekindle motivation. Your self-assurance allows you to pivot without feeling like you have failed.

---

13. Staying True to Your Values

13.1 Identifying Core Principles

As you grow older, clarifying your core values helps guide decisions. Maybe fairness, empathy, and continuous learning are crucial to you. When faced with moral or ethical dilemmas, these principles act like a compass. Consistently acting according to your values strengthens your confidence because you know you are being authentic.

13.2 Avoiding Peer Pressure in Adulthood

Peer pressure does not vanish after high school. It might show up in college fraternities, workplace gatherings, or social clubs. Remember the lessons from your teen years—your worth is not determined by going along with the crowd. If a situation feels wrong, you can walk away or propose an alternative that aligns better with your values.

13.3 Practicing Integrity in Work and Relationships

Lying, cheating, or taking unethical shortcuts might yield quick gains, but they corrode self-respect. Upholding honesty, fairness, and kindness can be difficult in competitive environments, but it ensures you keep faith in yourself. Over time, people who value authenticity will trust you more, leading to deeper, more stable connections.

13.4 Personal Mission Statements

Some individuals write short personal mission statements—like "I aim to be a supportive friend, a diligent learner, and a fair contributor to my community." Refer to it when you feel confused about a major choice. If an option goes against your mission statement, it is easier to refuse. This clarity can keep your confidence intact during complex decisions.

---

14. Adapting and Evolving

14.1 Embracing New Interests

Even if you settle on a major or career, remain open to fresh possibilities. You might stumble upon a new hobby at age 25 or decide to switch fields at 30. Life is not static. Growing confidence means trusting yourself to handle changes, even if that involves learning from scratch again.

14.2 Challenges as Stepping Stones

Adult life might throw unexpected issues—health scares, job layoffs, or personal losses. These experiences, though tough, can become moments where you prove your resilience. Remind yourself of past obstacles you overcame. Each victory, small or large, can reaffirm your faith in your adaptability.

14.3 Continuous Self-Reflection

Schedule periodic check-ins with yourself. Ask: "Am I still on track with my values and goals?" or "What lessons have I learned recently?" Self-reflection keeps you from running on autopilot and helps you spot emerging problems before they escalate.

14.4 Role Models at Different Stages

As a teen, you might have looked up to certain teachers, celebrities, or community leaders. In adulthood, you can find new role models—colleagues who excel at teamwork, entrepreneurs who balance profit with ethics, or activists championing important causes. Learning from diverse role models can keep your motivation fresh and broaden your perspective.

---

15. Celebrating Who You Have Become

15.1 Recognizing Your Journey

Take a moment to look back. Recall the self-doubts you had as a younger teen, the challenges you faced, and the skills you developed. Each obstacle overcame, each skill learned, contributed to the person you are today. This realization can fill you with gratitude and self-respect, important elements in maintaining a bright future outlook.

15.2 Sharing Your Story

If you feel comfortable, share parts of your life story with those who might be in a similar spot you were once in—maybe younger relatives or new peers in college. Hearing your challenges and how you tackled them can inspire someone else. It also cements your own confidence, as you see how far you have come.

15.3 Planning Periodic "Checkpoints"

Life does not hand you neat markers to say, "You have reached success." Instead, create your own checkpoints—maybe finishing a significant project, traveling to a place on your bucket list, or developing a new skill. Recognize these moments. Each checkpoint can be a reminder that progress is ongoing, not a single destination.

15.4 Being Proud of Your Uniqueness

Over time, you may realize your path is nothing like your friends' or what the media portrays. That is okay. Your uniqueness is an asset. Embrace your quirky interests, the combination of experiences that shaped you, and your personal style of living. True confidence often emerges when you stop trying to fit into someone else's mold and stand comfortably in your own.

www.ingramcontent.com/pod-product-compliance
Lightning Source LLC
LaVergne TN
LVHW012040070526
838202LV00056B/5548